NOTES
ON
INDIAN HISTORY
(664-1858)

NOTES

ON

INDIAN HISTORY

(664-1858)

KARL MARX

GYAN

Published by

Gyan Publishing House
5, Ansari Road
Daryaganj, New Delhi-110002
Phone: 011-47034999, 9811692060
E-mail: books@gyanbooks.com

Distribution Network
gyanbooks.com
India, USA, Canada, UK, Australia, France

ISBN: 978-81-212-8742-5 (PB)
First Published, 1900

2nd Impression 2023

Printed at: Gyan Press, Delhi.

NOTES ON INDIAN HISTORY (664-1858)
Author: Karl Marx

Karl Marx

KARL

MARX

NOTES ON INDIAN HISTORY (664-1858)

SECOND IMPRESSION

FOREIGN LANGUAGES PUBLISHING HOUSE
Moscow

PUBLISHER'S NOTE

This English edition of *Notes on Indian History* (*Chronologische Auszüge über Ostindien*) by Karl Marx follows the composition of the Russian edition prepared by the Institute of Marxism-Leninism of the C.C., C.P.S.U. in 1947. Due account has been taken of the corrections made by the Institute in the course of its subsequent work on the manuscript.

Unlike the Russian edition, insertions by the author are enclosed in parentheses.

The MS. of Notes was never edited by the author. That is the reason why, in preparing them for publication, certain changes of a technical nature had to be made, changes which naturally affected also material quoted by Marx from English authors in English. Specifically, the following alterations have been made:

1. The spelling of most Indian proper names, borrowed by the author from the works of Elphinstone and Sewell, has been brought into line with modern authoritative sources. Preference has been given to the traditional spelling.

2. Articles, pronouns, auxiliary verbs and conjunctions have been inserted wherever called for, and obvious slips of the pen have been corrected.

CONTENTS

PREFACE TO THE RUSSIAN EDITION

From the fifties on, Marx carefully studied India as a colonial country where diverse forms and methods of colonial rule and plunder had been practised. He also took interest in India because she still retained, to a certain degree, relations peculiar to primitive communal society. "However changing the political aspect of India's past must appear, her social condition has remained unaltered since her remotest antiquity, until the first decennium of the 19th century," Marx wrote in 1853. ("The British Rule in India," *Selected Works*, English edition, Moscow, Vol. I, p. 348.)

Marx's *Notes* cover more than a thousand years of Indian history—from the mid-7th to the mid-19th century: from the first Moslem invasions to August 2, 1858, when the British Parliament passed the India Bill legalizing the annexation of that country.

The early period, ending in the middle of the 18th century, takes up less than one-third of *Notes*. The rest of the manuscript is devoted to the history of the British conquest of India.

Marx lists the Moslem dynasties which ruled in northern India, in the valleys of the Indus and the Ganges, and from there extended their conquests southwards. He deals in greater detail with the history of the Mogul Empire, which came into being in 1526 following the invasion of Baber, who traced his ancestry back to Tamerlane and Genghis Khan.

Before turning to notes on the history of the British conquest of India, Marx once again lists in brief the various foreign invasions of India, beginning with Alexander of Macedon, and surveys the various Indian states.

Notes on Indian History hold a prominent place among the manuscripts written by Marx in the last years of his life. It is an important supplement to the *Chronological Notes* on general history published as part of the *Marx and Engels Archives* (Vols. V-VIII).

As he studied the changing forms of land tenure in India, Marx compiled a chronology intended as a succinct description of the course of historical events on the vast territory of that country. He did not confine himself to the nature of the forms of land tenure but sought to study the concrete historical process as a whole. Among other things, he studied the circumstances under which Moslem law had influenced Indian land tenure, as well as the development of the feudal system in this particular case and the manner in which the British had conquered and oppressed India.

Subsequently Marx analyzed, step by step, the expansion of British rule in India. The conquest of India proceeded under the direction of the British East India Company, founded in the early 17th century as a tool of financiers, merchants, and aristocrats. Marx reveals the imperialist forms and methods of government which the British used in India,and portrays a long succession of British rulers of India.

In the section headed by Marx "Last Period, 1823-1858 (Extinction of the East India Company)," the author lists a series of wars of conquest which the British waged in India and neighbouring countries.

Marx's *Notes* show how the British colonial empire expanded as the result of ruthless exploitation of the peoples of India, and emphasize the economic and political consequences of British rule for those peoples.

Marx read an immense number of books to compile his *Notes*. With regard to the early period of Indian history—from the 7th to the mid-18th century—he drew chiefly on Elphinstone's *History of India*. For the chronology of the political history of the British conquest of India, he used *The Analytical History of India* by Robert Sewell (London, 1870).

In preparing *Notes on Indian History* for the press, some absolutely necessary corrections were made where the manuscript departs from generally accepted and indisputable data. In a number of cases concerning which later authoritative research furnishes facts that are at variance with Marx's dates, footnotes give other dates, with reference to the appropriate sources.

All the footnotes are by the Editors. Editorial insertions in the author's text are enclosed in square brackets.

Institute of Marxism-Leninism of the C.C., C.P.S.U.

NOTES ON INDIAN HISTORY
(664-1858)

[MUSSULMAN CONQUEST OF INDIA]

First Arab entry into India A. D. 664 (year 44 of the Hegira). Muhallab penetrated into Multan.

632. *Mohammed died.*

633. Arabs under *Abu Bekr* invaded *Syria*; they attacked *Persia*, which they crushed in *638*, driving Persian Shah beyond the Oxus; about the same time, *Egypt* conquered by *Amr*, one of the Caliph's lieutenants.

650. *Shah of Persia* sought to regain his realm, was defeated and killed; the Arabs took the whole country up to the Oxus. *Persia and India* now *separated* only by *Kabul in the north* and *Baluchistan in the south*, with *Afghanistan* between them.

664. *Arabs* [reached] *Kabul*; in the same year, *Muhallab*, an Arab general, *raided* India, advanced as far as *Multan*.

690. *Conquest of Kabul* completed by *Abdurrahman*; sent as general by *Hajaj*, Governor of *Basra*, on the Persian Gulf [at the mouth of the Shatt al Arab].

711. *Sind conquered* by *Muhammad Kasim* (*nephew to Hajaj*) (he sailed from *Basra*).

714. *Muhammad Kasim* murdered by *Caliph Walid* out of jealousy; thereby *signal* was given *for the downfall of Mohammedanism in Sind. Thirty years later, not an Arab remained behind.*—Mohammedanism made more rapid progress among the *Persians* than among the *Hindus* because there priest class was lowest and most degraded class, whereas in India it was the most powerful political agent in the Commonwealth. (*Elphinstone.*)

(I) MUSSULMAN DYNASTIES IN KHORASSAN

713. Arabs established in Transoxiana[1]. (In *670, they crossed* the Oxus, and somewhat later took *Bokhara* and *Samarkand* from the *Turkomans*); there was a great conflict at that time between the *families of Fatima* (Mohammed's sister) and *Abbas* (his uncle) for the office of *Caliphate* over this newly acquired territory; the winners were *Abbas' family*, and *Harun al Rashid* became the *5th caliph* of that race. He died in—

809—on his way to Transoxiana to quell a rebellion; his son *Mamun* re-established Arab dominion in Khorassan, and later became *Caliph in Baghdad* in place of his father; his minister, *Tahir*, revolted and—

821—*proclaimed himself independent Regent of Khorassan*, where his family ruled—

821-870—as the *Tahirid Dynasty*; then he was deposed by the *Saffarid* family.

872-903. *Saffarid Dynasty*; *Yakub*, its last member, defeated by the *House of Samani*.

903-999. *Samanid Dynasty*. Various members of this family, who had independent possessions in Transoxiana, crossed the Oxus to the Persian side and conquered a large territory there, but the *House of Buya* (also called *the Deilemites*), then in possession of the Caliphate of Baghdad, drove them back into Khorassan, where they remained.

961. Under *Abd-al-Malik*, 5th rex[2] of the House of Samani, a *Turki slave* named *Alptegin*, who had entered royal service as court jester, was finally appointed Governor of *Khorassan*; Abd-al-Malik died soon after, and *Alptegin*, in disfavour with the new king, fled with a picked band of followers to *Ghazni*, where he made himself Governor.

Sabuktegin, one of *Alptegin*'s slaves, succeeded the latter in favour at the court of Khorassan. *Ghazni* was only 200 miles from the Indian frontier, and *Jaipal, Raja of Lahore*, feeling uneasy about the proximity of a

---

[1] Modern historians use the Arabic name of that region, *Mawarannahr*.
[2] Ruler.

Moslem government, led army *against Ghazni*; compromise concluded; not kept by the Raja; thereupon *Sabuktegin* invaded India, marching through the Sulaiman Mts. Jaipal made confederacy with the *Rajas of Delhi*, *Kanauj*, and *Kalinjar*, advanced with army of several hundred thousand, and was *defeated by Sabuktegin*, who withdrew soon afterwards, leaving a *Mohammedan officer as Governor of Peshawar, in the Punjab*. Meanwhile a Tartar revolt had broken out against the Samanid King *Nuh*, 7th member of his family, and he was driven to the Persian side of the Oxus. Sabuktegin rushed to his aid, expelled the rebels, and out of gratitude Nuh made *Mahmud* (Sabuktegin's eldest son) *Governor of Khorassan*. As the latter was absent at Sabuktegin's death, the throne of Ghazni was seized by his *younger brother Ismail*; but Mahmud beat and imprisoned him. Mahmud sent an embassy to *Mansur*, then Samanid King, and demanded to be recognized as *Governor of Ghazni*; this was refused; *Mahmud* proclaimed himself *independent King of Ghazni*; *Mansur* was dethroned shortly afterwards and—

999—*Mahmud of Ghazni* assumed the title of *Sultan*

999-April 29, 1030 (*when he died*), Mahmud of Ghazni.

999. *Ilek Khan*, one of Mansur's chieftains, took advantage of the fall of the Samanids to seize *Bokhara* and all the Moslem possessions in Transoxiana. War between him and Mahmud.

1000. Mahmud made peace with Ilek Khan and married his daughter. His plan in so doing was to have freedom of action for expedition against India.

(2) MAHMUD OF GHAZNI, AND HIS INVASIONS OF INDIA; DITTO HIS DESCENDANTS, 999-1152, RESP. 1186

1001. *Mahmud's First Invasion of India. Lahore*. With large force Mahmud crossed the Sulaiman Mts.; attacked *Jaipal, Raja of Lahore, near Peshawar*; then crossed *Sutlej River*, taking *Bhatinda*; returned to Ghazni, leaving *Anand Pal*, Jaipal's son, as Raja.

1003. [1]Mahmud's Second Invasion. *Bhatia.* Anand Pal kept peace terms imposed on him, but one of the parties to the peace, the *Raja of Bhatia*, refused to pay tribute. Mahmud went against him and defeated him.

1005. *Mahmud's Third Invasion. Multan. Abul Fateh Lodi, Afghan Chief of Multan*, revolted; Mahmud defeated him and *imposed a contribution*. During his absence, *Ilek Khan* crossed the Oxus and attacked Khorassan with large Tartar army. Mahmud (with *Indian* elephants) hurried from *Ghazni* to Khorassan, drove Ilek Khan back to Bokhara.

1008. *Mahmud's Fourth Invasion. Punjab.* Temple of *Nagarkot. Anand Pal* of Bhatinda formed powerful combination of Indian chieftains against Mahmud. Hindus fought fanatically; Mahmud defeated them, sacked temple of Nagarkot.

1010. Mahmud conquered *Kingdom of Ghur, inhabited by the Afghans.*

Winter 1010. *Mahmud's Fifth Invasion. New invasion of Multan*, Abul Fateh Lodi brought to Ghazni as a prisoner.

1011. *Mahmud's Sixth Invasion. Thanesar* (on the Jumna); here he captured rich temple before the princes could gather their army.

1013 and 1014. *Seventh and Eighth Invasions.* In *Kashmir*, two predatory and reconnoitring incursions.

1013. *Ilek Khan died.* In *1016*, Mahmud took *Bokhara and Samarkand*, and in *1017* completed the conquest of Transoxiana.

Winter 1017. *Ninth Invasion.* Great invasion by Mahmud; he marched through *Peshawar into Kashmir*, thence to the *Jumna*, crossed it, *Kanauj* (ancient city) surrendered to him; he then went on to *Muttra*, which he razed to the ground; returned after *sacking Mahawan* and *Munj*.

1022. *Tenth and Eleventh Invasions.* Two campaigns in aid of the Raja of Kanauj, who was expelled from this city. During one of these expeditions, *Lahore absolutely reduced.*

---

[1] 1004, according to Elphinstone, *The History of India*, London, 1866.

1024. *Twelfth Invasion. Gujarat and Somnath.* Mahmud's last great expedition; he marched from Ghazni to Multan, then across the *Sind Desert to Gujarat*, took the capital, *Anhalwar*, on his way devastated the *territories of the Raja of Ajmer*, then captured the *temple of Somnath*, gallantly defended by Rajput garrison. Then Mahmud returned to Anhalwar, where he stayed for a year. His [withdrawal] through the desert was disastrous.

1027. The Turki tribe of the *Seljuks* revolted, was crushed by Mahmud.

1028. *The whole of Persia* brought under Mahmud's rule through reconquest of Persian *Iraq* from the Deilemites.

April 29, 1030. *Death of Mahmud of Ghazni.* The poet *Firdausi* lived at his court. His army consisted mainly of *Turks*, who were considered slaves to the Persians and formed into regiments of *Mameluke* (slave) *Guards.* The *shepherds* were mostly Tartars. The *nobles* and *bulk of the higher population* were *Arabs*; they had all *powers of justice and religion*; *civil government* was mostly carried on by the *Persians.*

Mahmud left three sons: *Muhammad, Mas'ud,* and *Abul Rashid*; when dying, he appointed the eldest, *Muhammad,* to be Sultan, but in the same year (1030) *Mas'ud,* a favourite of the soldiers, caught his elder brother, blinded him, held him captive, and took possession of the throne.

1030-1041. *Sultan Mas'ud I.* Under him the Seljuk Turks beyond the Oxus rose in revolt; Mas'ud drove them back to their country.

1034. *Mas'ud I* [went] to India to quell unrest at Lahore, then marched against the Seljuks.

1034-1039. His war against the Seljuks; he was utterly defeated at *Zendegan* [Dandankan], near *Merv,* and fled to India; mutiny of his officers; they placed on throne Muhammad's son *Ahmed,* who had his uncle Mas'ud pursued, seized, and—

1041—*put to death. Sultan Ahmed* [attacked] by *Maudud,* son of the murdered Sultan. [He] set out from Balkh, met Ahmed at Laghman, defeated him, had him and the whole of his family put to death, and proclaimed himself Sultan.

1041-1050. *Sultan Maudud.* Seljuks in Transoxiana elected *Toghrul Beg* their leader, sought conquests in all directions, and scattered their force, so that Maudud was enabled to conquer Transoxiana.—On the other hand, *King of Delhi* rebelled, wrested from the Mohammedans Thanesar, Nagarkot, and all the territory beyond the Sutlej except *Lahore*, saved by small Mohammedan garrison.

1046. *Maudud*, who had fought against the Seljuks all his life, was asked by the *Raja of Ghur* to help him against that tribe, promised to do so, but instead murdered his ally and took possession of *Ghur*; he himself *died in 1050 at Ghazni*; was succeeded by his younger brother—

1050-1051—*Sultan Abul Hasan*; the whole country rebelled against him; he was left with nothing but Ghazni. His general, *Ali Ibn Rabia*, went to India, where he made conquests on his own account. The entire West [rose up] in arms for the Sultan's uncle, *Abul Rashid*, youngest son of Sultan Mahmud; the latter deposed Abul Hasan at Ghazni.

1051-1052. *Sultan Abul Rashid*; besieged at Ghazni by the rebel chief, *Toghrul*, the fort stormed and Sultan with nine royal princes murdered; Toghrul murdered by the infuriated populace and his tribe expelled. The country searched for some prince of House of *Sabuktegin*; *Farrukhzad*, imprisoned *in a fort*, found, released, and set on throne.

1052-1058. *Sultan Farrukhzad.* Peaceful reign; died natural death; succeeded by his brother—

1058-1089—*Sultan Ibrahim* (the Pious). Uneventful reign; succeeded by *his son*—

1089-1114—*Sultan Mas'ud II*; *he carried the Mohammedan arms beyond the Ganges*; succeeded by his son—

1114-1118—*Sultan Arslan*; he seized and imprisoned all his brothers, except *Bahram*, who escaped by fleeing to the *Seljuks*; these took up his cause, marched against Arslan, defeated him, and set Bahram on the throne.

1118-1152. *Sultan Bahram.* After some years' reign, he interfered with *Ghur*, put one of the princes to death; *Saifuddin*, brother of the murdered man, rose against him, took Ghazni, and drove Bahram into the mountains. *Bahram came back*, seized Saifuddin, tortured him to death; *Ala-uddin*, a brother of the slaughtered man, came with army of Ghurians, utterly destroyed Ghazni, razed it to the ground, spared only three buildings—the tombs of Mahmud, Mas'ud I, and Ibrahim. *Bahram fled to Lahore*, and the *Ghaznevid Dynasty* came to an end. The royal *family of Ghazni* ruled at *Lahore for 34 years* more (*till 1186*), became then extinct. Thus ended the *Dynasty of Mahmud of Ghazni, 187 years* after Mahmud had proclaimed himself Sultan (in 999.)

(3) HOUSE OF GHUR, ESTABLISHING ITSELF AT GHAZNI ON THE RUINS OF THE HOUSE OF SABUKTEGIN, 1152-1206

1152-1156. *Ala-uddin.* Bahram, in escaping from Arslan to the Seljuks, had promised to pay them *tribute* if they restored him to the throne, and actually paid it till his expulsion. *As soon as Ala-uddin* proclaimed himself King of Ghazni, *Sanjar*, the Seljuk chief, demanded that the tribute should be paid as before; Ala-uddin refused, Sanjar led his army against him and took him prisoner; nevertheless, he reinstated him.

1153. *Tartar tribe of the Oghuz* overran the territories of both *Sanjar* and *Ala-uddin*. At his death the latter was succeeded by his son—

1156-1157—*Saifuddin*; he was killed by one of his nobles, whose brother he had murdered. There were *two nephews of Ala-uddin*, the brothers *Ghiyasuddin* and *Shehabuddin.*

1157-1202. *Ghiyasuddin* on throne, made his brother Shehab commander of the armies and allied himself with him. The two brothers *conquered Khorassan from the Seljuks*, and worked harmoniously together.

1176. *Shehab* [went] to *Lahore*, defeated *Khusrau II, last representative of the House of Mahmud.*

1181. *Shehab took Sind*, and in *1186* imprisoned Khusrau; then he turned his attention to the powerful *Rajput principalities* in Hindustan; defeated, in attack on *Delhi*, by the great *Raja Prithwi*, who at that time ruled over Delhi and Ajmer, he returned to Ghazni.

1193. *Shehab* invaded India again, defeated Raja Prithwi, killed him, left *Kutbuddin*, an ennobled slave,[1] as *Governor of Ajmer*. The latter *captured Delhi*, remained there as Governor, and later proclaimed himself independent, becoming the *first Mohammedan King of Delhi*.

1194. *Shehab* took *Kanauj and Benares* (the *Raja of the former city* [was killed] *and his family* driven *to Marwar*, where they established a principality), annexed also *Gwalior*, while *Kutbuddin* ravaged *Gujarat*, *Oudh*, *North Bihar*, and *Bengal*.

1202. *Ghiyas died*; succeeded by his brother—

1202-1206—*Shehabuddin*; attempted conquest of *Khwarezm*, was defeated and had to flee for his life.

1206. *His second march on Khwarezm*; murdered by some *Kakars* (a robber tribe) when separated from his escort; succeeded by his nephew—

1206—*Mahmud*; was unable to safeguard kingdom against internal dissensions; it fell to pieces; its various parts fell into the hands of Shehab's favourite slaves. *Partition of the sultanate*: *Kutbuddin* took Delhi and the Indian possessions. (*Delhi* had been the capital of a kingdom, a small and insignificant one, for *1,200 years*.) *Yildiz*, a slave, took *Ghazni*, but was expelled by the King of Khwarezm, and fled to Delhi. *Nazirud-din*, another slave, made himself master of *Multan and Sind*.

((4) THE SLAVE [MAMELUKE] KINGS OF DELHI, 1206-1288

1206-1210. *Kutbuddin*; succeeded on his death by his son—

1210—*Aram*, who in the following year was *overthrown* and supplanted by his brother-in law—

[1] The slaves (Mamelukes) of an Eastern ruler often played a prominent role at court, and sometimes led palace revolutions.

1211-1236—*Shamsuddin Altamsh.*

1217. *Enormous army of Mongols under Genghis Khan* (b. 1164[1]), coming from Turan, *attacked Khwarezm*, gallantly defended by *Jalal* [the Shah's son] as far as the banks of the Indus, whither he was pushed. As none of the princes supported him, fearing the Mongols, he collected a *band of Kakars*, and plundered far and wide. Then *Genghis Khan* sent large army into Naziruddin's *territory of Multan and Sind* and ravaged them; when the Mongols had withdrawn across the Indus, *Shamsuddin Altamsh* took advantage of the condition of the country to *attack, conquer, and annex* it.

1225. *Shamsuddin* conquered *Bihar* and *Malwa*, and was—

1232—recognized as King *throughout Hindustan proper*; he died in *1236* at the zenith of his power, and was succeeded—

1236—by *his son Rukneddin*; in the same year he was deposed by his *sister*! who seized throne.

1236-1239. *Sultana Razia*; her love affair with an Abyssinian slave at the court outraged court nobles; *Altunia, Chief of Bhatinda*, revolted, took her prisoner, she fell in love with him and married him; he then led army to Delhi; nobles defeated him, put her to death; she was succeeded by *her brother*—

1239-1241—*Muizzuddin Bahram*, terrible despot; he was murdered; succeeded by *Rukneddin*'s son—

1241-1246—*Ala-uddin Mas'ud*; assassinated. Throne now went to a grandson of *Shamsuddin Altamsh and son of Muizzuddin Bahram*—

1246-1266—*Naziruddin Mahmud.* Slave named *Ghiyasuddin Balban* was his minister; this Balban *formed powerful border confederacy to repel Mogul* (*Mongol*) *attacks*, and defeated many of the minor Hindu states.

1258. Balban repelled another Mongol attack on Punjab.

1266. King *Naziruddin Mahmud* died without issue; throne went to his minister—

1266-1286—*Ghiyasuddin Balban*; his court was the only *Mohammedan court* in India.

---

[1] In Marx's chronological excerpts from Schlosser, the year of Genghis Khan's birth is given as 1155 (*Marx and Engels Archives*, Vol. V, p. 219). This date is now generally accepted.

1279. He took the field because of insurrection in Bengal; during his absence *Toghrul, the Governor of Delhi,* revolted and made himself sovereign of that city; coming back, *Ghiyas* defeated him, killed him and 100,000 prisoners; he died in *1286,* and was *succeeded, not by his second son* (his first son had died earlier), *Bakarra Khan,* who was still alive, but by the latter's son—

1286-1288—Kaikobad (the eldest son of Balban, Muhammad, had likewise left a son, *Kaikhusrau,* who was appointed (*Governor of Multan*).

1287. [Kaikobad] poisoned his intriguing Vizier, *Nizamuddin* (who at first plotted with *Kaikhusrau,* then had him put to death; he had also persuaded Kaikobad to treacherously murder *all the Mongols at his court* during a banquet). On the Vizier's death, confusion at the court. Chief party in Delhi at that time (1287) was that of the *old Ghaznevid family* of the *Khiljies;* in *1288,* they killed *Kaikobad* and—

1288—set their leader, *Jalaluddin Khilji,* on *throne of Delhi.*

(5) HOUSE OF KHILJI, 1288-1321

1288-1295. *Jalaluddin Khilji;* introduced mild regime; pardoned a rebel chief, nephew of Ghiyasuddin; on beating back a *Mongol incursion,* he released all the prisoners.

1293. *3,000 Mongols* joined him, and were settled at Delhi. His nephew *Ala-uddin,* made Governor of Oudh, planned *invasion of the Deccan,* marched through *Ellichpur* to *Deogiri* (now called *Daulatabad*), took the Hindu Raja living in profound peace by surprise, plundered his city and treasures, and imposed indemnity on the surrounding country; the *Raja made peace with him* and he returned to *Malwa;* then he went to *Delhi,* where he stabbed his royal uncle to the heart as the latter was embracing him.

1295-1317. *Ala-uddin Khilji* (most ferocious and sanguinary). At his uncle's death, he killed the latter's sons and widow. This led to rising, crushed by him through wholesale massacre of the rebels' women and children.

1297. He conquered *Gujarat*. Shortly afterwards [came] a *Mongol invasion*, repelled by *Ala-uddin*.

1298.[1] While on a hunting expedition, *Ala-uddin* was wounded by his nephew, Prince *Suleiman*, who left him behind as dead. *Suleiman* [went] to Delhi and laid claim to the throne; but *Ala-uddin*, having recovered, appeared before the army, which rallied to him *en masse*. *Suleiman and two other nephews beheaded*; thereupon popular uprising, quelled by terrible displays of cruelty.

1303. *Ala-uddin took Chitor in Mewar*, one of the most renowned hill forts in India, from a rebellious *Rajput*; ditto, *Mongol incursion*.

1304. *Mongols made three separate attempts* to force an entrance into Hindustan; each time repulsed; according to *Ferishtah*, on these occasions *all the Mongol prisoners brought into camp* were butchered in cold blood.

1306. *As the Raja of Deogiri* refused to pay the tribute imposed on him by Jalaluddin, *Ala-uddin* sent large army under the *eunuch* and former slave, *Malik Kafur*. The Raja was defeated and taken to Delhi, where he spent the rest of his life.

1309. *Malik Kafur* was sent south again, this time to *Telingana*, where he was victorious, capturing the strong fortress of Warangal.

1310. *Malik Kafur* conquered *Carnata* and the *entire eastern coast to Cape Comorin*, returned to Delhi, loaded with treasures; he had built mosque at Cape Comorin to commemorate the extension of his conquests. This was the *first Mohammedan invasion of Tamil soil*. *Ala-uddin* massacred all the 15,000 Moguls living at Delhi. *Malik Kafur* began to plot for succession; great disorder in the country because the people outraged by Ala-uddin's ferocity and tyranny.

1316. After the "tyrant" had given up the ghost in a fit of apoplexy brought on by rage, Kafur sought to seize the throne, but was "done in," and was succeeded by Ala-uddin's son—

1317-1320—*Mubarak Khilji*; he began by blinding his third brother and murdering the two generals who had

---

[1] 1299, according to Elphinstone.

helped him to the throne; then he disbanded his whole army, made a slave—*Khusrau Khan*—his *Vizier*, and gave himself up to degrading debaucheries.

1319. *Khusrau* conquered *Malabar*, returned—

1320—to Delhi, killed King *Mubarak*, and freed the country from *the Khiljies* by finishing off all their survivors; he then seized the throne; but—

1321—a large *army* coming from the Punjab under *Ghiyasuddin Tughlak*, Governor of that province, appeared *before Delhi*; *Delhi* was sacked, Khusrau "done in," and the ex-Governor became King and founder of the House of *Tughlak*, which ruled in Delhi for more than 100 years. *Ghiyasuddin Tughlak* was *the son of a slave of* (*ex-slave*) *Ghiyasuddin Balban*, Vizier and successor of *Naziruddin Mahmud*.

(6) HOUSE OF TUGHLAK, 1321-1414

1321-1325. *Ghiyasuddin Tughlak I*; extremely mild reign.

1324. He undertook an expedition to *Bengal*, leaving his son *Juna Khan* to govern. On his return—

1325—he was killed by a falling pavilion during court festivities; succeeded by his son *Juna Khan* under the name of—

1325-1351—*Muhammad Tughlak*; the ablest prince of his time, he ruined himself by his own much too extensive plans. *His first action*: he bought off the Mongols and conciliated them so far that they made no incursions throughout his reign. Then he *reduced Deccan to submission*. After that [came] his schemes of universal empire.

[He] formed so vast an "*Army of Persia*" (to conquer the latter) that he fell short of money to pay it; then he proposed to subdue *China*, and sent 100,000 men to find a passage through the Himalayas; they lost their lives, almost to a man, in the *tarai*[1] jungles. As his treasury was empty, he imposed *most ruinous exactions on the people*; *taxes were so heavy* that the

[1] Wooded foothills.

poor fled to the forests; he drew a *cordon of troops* round these and then had the fugitives slaughtered in a grand battue in which he took part, riding the men down like game. Result: *total failure of crops* and a *terrible famine*. Rebellions broke out on all parts; those in *Malwa and the Punjab* were easily put down, but—

1340—*rebellion in Bengal was successful.* The *Coromandel Coast* (eastern coast of India from River Kistna to Cape Comorin) revolted and won freedom. *Telingana* and *Carnata* revolted successfully. The *Afghans ravaged the Punjab*, *Gujarat* rebelled, and famine was at its height. The King [marched] on Gujarat, ravaged the whole province, and then hurried about the country, trying to suppress each rebellion in turn; while at it—

1351—he died of fever in *Tatta, Sind.* (*Elphinstone* says in *The History of India*: "*There is in general so little scruple about getting rid of a bad king in the East that it is seldom such extensive mischief is brought about by the misgovernment of one man.*") He was succeeded by his nephew—

1351-1388—*Firuz Tughlak*; after futile attempt to *recover Bengal*, he recognized the *independence of that province* and of the *Deccan*; unimportant reign of slight rebellions and slight wars.

1385. Too old to rule, he appointed a Vizier.

1386. he made his son *Naziruddin* King in his place; but the ex-King's *nephews*—

1387—expelled Nazir from Delhi, declaring that *Firuz* had abdicated in favour of his grandson *Ghiyasuddin; Firuz* d. 1388, at the age of 90.

1388-1389. *Ghiyasuddin Tughlak II*; at once quarrelled with the cousins who had elevated him to the throne, was deposed by them soon after; the throne went to *his brother*—

1389-1390—*Abu Bakr Tughlak*; his uncle Nazir marched on Delhi with a large army, and took him prisoner.

1390-1394. *Naziruddin Tughlak* died after four years' reign; his eldest son *Humayun caroused himself to death* during his 45 days' reign, was succeeded by *his brother*—

1394-1414—*Mahmud Tughlak.* Revolts, factions, wars. *Malwa, Gujarat, and Khandesh* at once shook off submission. Even *Delhi* was the scene of continuous fights and disturbances between the groups [when]—

1398—[came] *Timur's* (*Tamerlane's*) *first invasion* (after he had overrun and subdued very nearly the whole of Genghis Khan's empire, then *overrun Persia, Transoxiana, Tartary, and Siberia*). *Timur* entered [India] *via Kabul*, while his grandson *Pir Muhammad* attacked *Multan*. The two armies joined on the Sutlej and *advanced on Delhi*, devastating the country on their way. *Mahmud Tughlak* fled to *Gujarat*; meanwhile *Delhi* was sacked and burned, and its inhabitants were massacred. Then the Mongols took *Meerut* and—

1399—returned by way of Kabul to Transoxiana, loaded with spoil. Mahmud then came back to Delhi, where he *died in 1414*. Tamerlane had left as Governor *Khizr Khan*, who proclaimed himself sovereign under the name of *the Sayyid*, or *lineal descendant of the Prophet*, the same word as *seid* or *sidi*, *mot arabe* qui veut dire le *seigneur*,[1] same as *Cid*, honorary title assumed by all who claim to be descended from Mohammed; il est porté aussi par tous les *Ismaéliens*.[2]

(7) GOVERNMENT OF THE SAYYIDS, 1414-1450

1414-1421. *Sayyid Khizr Khan*; *nothing was left of Kingdom of Delhi but the city and a small territory around*, all of *Ala-uddin Khilji's acquisitions having been lost*. *Khizr Khan* played role of a mere deputy acting for Timur, was indeed a petty little monarch. He effected *a levy of tribute on Rohilkhand and Gwalior*; succeeded by his son—

1421-1436—*Sayyid Mubarak*. A great deal of disturbance in the Punjab, he was not concerned. *Was murdered by his Vizier in 1436*; succeeded by his son—

1436-1444—*Sayyid Muhammad*; territory of Delhi invaded by *King of Malwa*; the Sayyid beat him back, calling the Governor of the Punjab, *Bahlol Khan Lodi*, to his aid; succeeded by his son—

---

[1] *Arabic word* meaning *lord*.

[2] It is also borne by all *Ishmaelites*.

1444-1450—*Sayyid Ala-uddin*; he moved his residency to *Budaun*, beyond the Ganges; *Bahlol Khan Lodi, Governor of the Punjab*, took possession of Delhi.

(8) HOUSE OF LODI, 1450-1526

1450-1488. *Bahlol Lodi; he united Punjab with Delhi. In 1452, the Raja of Jaunpur laid siege to Delhi, which led to war that lasted for 26 years* (this is important; it shows that the native Indian princes had become powerful enough [to oppose] the old Moslem rule) and ended in the total defeat of the Raja and *annexation of Jaunpur to Delhi*. Bahlol made further conquests; at his death the *realm comprised the land from the Jumna to the Himalayas, eastwards to Benares, westwards to Bundelkhand*. Succeeded by his son—

1488-1506—*Sikandar Lodi*; he *re-annexed Bihar*; an able and peaceful sovereign; succeeded by his son—

1506-1526—*Ibrahim Lodi*; ferocious; *murdered all the chiefs at court*; attempted the same proceeding against the *Governor of Punjab*; *the latter called the Moguls under Baber to his aid.*

1524. *Baber's invasion of India*; Baber imprisoned the Governor of the Punjab who had called him, took *Lahore* where *Ala-uddin, brother of Ibrahim of Delhi*, joined him, *and at head of Mogul army was sent to conquer Delhi*. Ibrahim utterly routed him; then Baber came himself; the two armies met at *Panipat* (near the *Jumna, north of Delhi*).

1526. *First Battle of Panipat*. Ibrahim was defeated, he himself and *40,000 Hindus* remained on battlefield. *Baber occupied Delhi and Agra.*

. . . .

Robert Sewell (Madras Civil Service) says in *The Analytical History of India* (*1870*):

Three big races in Asia: (1) *Turks* (Turkomans), living about *Bokhara* and westwards to the *Caspian Sea*; (2) *Tartars*, inhabiting part of Siberia and Russia, with their main tribes in *Astrakhan* and *Kazan* and over-spreading the whole country *north of the Turki tribes*; (3) *Moguls, or Mongols*, occupying *Mongolia, Tibet, and Manchuria*; *shepherd tribes* all. *Western Moguls, or Kalmucks*, and *eastern Moguls*, divided into many tribes, or *ulus*. These *ulus*, or *clans*, frequently united under one leader by a sort of mutual alliance.

1164. *Genghis Khan born*; chief of insignificant clan paying tribute to the Khitan Tartars; plus tard[1] the Tartars joined his armies after he had thrashed them, and his host outnumbered the Mongols. With this force *Genghis Khan* conquered Eastern Mongolia and North China, then Transoxiana and Khorassan; he conquered the Turki country, i.e., *Bokhara, Khwarezm, Persia*, and invaded India. At that time his empire extended from the *Caspian Sea* to *Peking*, southwards to the Indian Ocean and the Himalayas, Astrakhan and Kazan being western boundary. On his death his empire was divided into four parts: *Kipchak, Iran, Jagatai, and Mongolia with China*; the three first governed by khans; the ruler of the last, as being the original dominant country, was *Supreme*, or *Great, Khan*.

1336. *Timur* born in *Kesh, Jagatai*, not far from Samarkand; he succeeded—

1360—*his uncle Saifuddin as Prince of Kesh* and chieftain of the Barulas tribe, under the suzerainty of *Tughlak Timur*, Khan of Jagatai.

1370. Tamerlane took possession of that khanate, etc. He died in *1405*. After his death his empire was divided among his sons; the largest share went to *Pir Muhammad*, second son of Timur's eldest son.

According to same author (*Sewell*), principal families of the Turks were the *Ottomans* (they moved westwards in the 14th century, establishing their power in *Phrygia*, whence they were never expelled), the *Seljuks* (mainly in *Persia, Syria, and Iconium*), and the *Uzbeks*

[1] Later.

(*arose in 1305*); these were *Kipchak Turks*, and derived the name *Uzbek* from their Khan, *b. 1305* They wielded great power in Baber's time.[1]

1526. *Baber, sixth in descent from Timur (Tamerlane); he was son of Omar Sheik Mirza, King of Ferghana (province of present-day Kokand).* Sole *Mogul monarch* who wrote his own *biography*; it was translated by *Leyden and Erskine* (1826). *B. 1483, d. 1530.*

. . . .

States of India at the Time of Baber's Arrival

1351. *With break-up of the Delhi Kingdom of Muhammad Tughlak,* various new states came into being. *About 1398 (at the time of Timur's invasion), the whole of India,* except *a few miles round Delhi,* was *free from Mohammedan domination*; the chief Indian states were:

(1) *Bahmani Kings of the Deccan*; founded by a poor man named *Gangu Bahmani*, who rose to independence at *Gulbarga*.

1421. The *Bahmani King* expelled the [Raja of] *Telingana*
Hindu from *Warangal* (Telingana comprised the provinces of the Northern *Circars, Hyderabad—Balaghat, Carnatic*. The *langue telinga*[2] still spoken between Ganjam and Pulicat), and later took *Rajahmundry, Masulipatam*, and *Conjeeveram*. Soon after, internal commotions through [the enmity of] the two religious sects of *Shiahs* and *Sunnis*; the [former], under *Yusuf Adil*,

---

[1] Robert Sewell's book contains a number of inaccuracies. First, he affirms that the Siberian Tartars and the Mongols are two different peoples. Second—see p. 22 for the date of birth of Genghis Khan. Third, on Timur's death, it was his son Shahrud, the ruler of Khorassan, Seistan, and Mazanderan, who attained to the greatest power, and not Pir Muhammad, as Sewell affirms. Fourth, the migration of the Ottoman Turks from Central Asia to Asia Minor is questioned by many historians. In the 14th century, the Ottomans rose to power in the area about Bursa, whence they extended their authority to the surrounding country. Fifth, speaking of the Uzbeks, Sewell mentions Uzbek Khan, who ruled over the Golden Horde from 1313 to 1340. The name *Uzbek* was borrowed from him by a section of the Yuehchi tribes, who adopted Islam at his instance.

[2] Telinga, or Telugu, language.

went to *Bijapur* and founded a kingdom, calling their leader King *Adil Shah.*

(2) *Bijapur-Ahmadnagar.*

1489-1579,[1] *period of reign of the dynasty.* It was in this small kingdom that the *Marathas* arose, and a famous Brahmin, withdrawing from here with his disciples, founded the Kingdom of *Ahmadnagar.*

(3) *Golconda*[2]*-Berar-Bidar.* These three small states arose in much the same manner, and *lasted till the late 16th century.*

(4) *Gujarat (1351-1388). Under Firuz Tughlak, Muzaffar Shah, a Rajput,* was appointed its *Governor*; he made it into an independent state. Later his successors annexed *Malwa* after hard fighting (1531). This kingdom lasted *from 1396 to 1561.*[3]

(5) *Malwa* became independent simultaneously with Gujarat, was ruled by a *Ghurian* family *till 1531,* when *Bahadur Shah* of Gujarat annexed it permanently.

(6) *Khandesh*; became independent state in *1399*, reannexed to Delhi by Akbar in *1599.*

(7) *Rajput States.* Several Rajput states in central India,
Hindu generally formed of wild mountain tribes, magnificent soldiers; the more important of them were: *Chitor, Marwar* (or *Jodhpur*), *Bikaner, Jaisalmer, Jaipur.*

---

[1] Marx here gives the time when the last representative of the dynasty began to rule. His reign ended in 1595.

[2] From the late 16th century on, Golconda virtually depended on Bijapur, having lost much of its political importance. It became a vassal of the Mogul Empire only in 1636, and was finally annexed to it in 1687.

[3] Marx here gives the year when the last representative of the dynasty began to rule. His reign ended in 1572.

THE MOGUL EMPIRE IN INDIA, 1526-1761[1]
(Lasted 235 Years)

(1) REIGN OF BABER

1526-1530. *Reign of Baber.*
1526. Within a few months, Baber's *eldest son Humayun* subdued the whole of the territory held by Ibrahim Lodi.
1527. *Sangram, King of Mewar*, a *Rajput prince*, who had brought *Ajmer and Malwa* under his rule and was *recognized as feudatory leader of Marwar and Jaipur*, led a large army against the Delhi State; [he] took *Biana* near *Agra* and defeated a unit of Baber's force. *Battle of Sikri ("the Indian Hastings")*.[2] Big victory of Baber, who established his power in India. (In his later battles, Baber used gunpowder along with arrows; he mentions his *mortars* and *matchlockmen*, and his *bowmen*; was himself a fine shot with bow and arrow.)
1528. *Chanderi* (*Chendari*; *Sindhia*), belonging to a *Rajput* prince, was taken with great loss, the whole garrison being killed to a man. At the same time, *Humayun* was beaten by the Afghans in Oudh; Baber marched from Chanderi to his assistance, defeated the enemy,

[1] The so-called *Mogul Empire* was founded by Baber in 1526 and lasted till 1761. Baber called himself a "Mogul" (distortion of "Mongol") as one who was supposed to be descended (in the sixth generation) from the famous Tamerlane, and from Genghis Khan on his mother's side. In reality neither he, who came from Persia, nor his army, which consisted of Turks, Persians, and Afghans, were Mongols. The official language of the Mogul Empire was Persian. On the death of Aurangzeb in 1707, the empire vi.tually began to disintegrate, although the Great Mogul, or Emperor, stripped of all authority, retained the throne of Delhi till 1857.

[2] In that battle the Moslem Moguls' troops defeated the Hindu troops and conquered India.

and returned to Delhi. Soon afterwards, [son of] *Sangram* surrendered the fortress *Rantambhor*.

1529. Hearing that *Mahmud Lodi* had taken *Bihar*, *Baber* marched against him, routed him, and *annexed his territories*; he then beat the *King of Bengal* (who held *North Bihar*) *at the fords of the Gogra River*, and finished the campaign by decimating a *tribe of half-wild Afghans*, who had seized Lahore.

December 26, 1530. *Baber* died of fever at Delhi, was buried at *Kabul* in compliance with his wish, at a spot chosen by him for the purpose, a *holiday resort of the Kabul people* to this day. (See *Burnes.*)

(2) FIRST AND SECOND REIGN OF HUMAYUN, WITH THE INTERMEDIATE GOVERNMENT OF THE HOUSE OF SUR, 1530-1556

1530. *Baber left four sons*: *Humayun*, Emperor (his successor); *Kamran*, then Governor of *Kabul*, proclaimed himself independent after his father's death; *Hindal* was Governor of *Sambhal*; and *Mirza Askari*, an intrepid soldier, of *Mewat*. *Humayun's first action* was to quell rebellion in *Jaunpur* (Chanpur); [he] then waged war against *Gujarat*, whose King, *Bahadur Shah*, on receiving the news of Baber's death, had declared war on the Moguls. *In the course of five years*, i.e., by—

1535—*Humayun* had destroyed *the army of Gujarat*; he then took *Champanir*, fort to which *Bahadur* had retired.

1536. *That fort was soon captured*, and Bahadur feigned reconciliation with him.

1537. *Humayun* being actively engaged against *Sher Khan*, who was operating against *Bengal*, *Bahadur Shah* retook *Gujarat* and *attacked Malwa*.

1537-1540. *Humayun's Campaigns Against Sher Khan. Sher Khan*, alias *Sher Shah*, *was a descendant of the Ghurian kings of Delhi*.

1527. after overthrowing the Lodis, he joined *Baber's army* as an officer, distinguished himself, Baber entrusted him with a command in Bihar.

1529. *Mahmud Lodi* took Bihar, and Sher Khan joined him; on Mahmud's death he became master of *Bihar.*

1532. when Humayun was in Gujarat, *Sher Shah* advanced into Bengal, therefore—

1537—*Humayun* set out with army against him; there, despite the manoeuvres of both—

1539—in camp on Ganges, *Humayun* was *surprised by Sher Shah, thoroughly worsted, had to flee*, while *Sher Khan*, alias *Sher Shah*, seized Bengal.

1540. *Humayun* took initiative by *marching on Kanauj*; was defeated again, almost drowned in Ganges during his flight; *Sher Khan* pursued him to *Lahore*; Humayun escaped to *Sind*; after one or two fruitless sieges, he fled to *Marwar* (Jodhpur), but Raja refused to admit him, and he tramped in the *deserts of Jaisalmer*, where his and his few followers' *encampments* were attacked continuously; there—

October 14, 1542—*Hamida, a dancing girl* of great beauty in his harem, gave birth to the *famous Akbar*; after roaming the desert for 18 months, they arrived at *Omercote* (*Umarkot*), where they were hospitably received. After another futile attempt to *reduce Sind*, *Humayun* was allowed to go to *Kandahar*; found that province in the hands of his brother *Mirza Askari*, who refused to help him. *Humayun* fled to *Herat* (*Persia*). In Persia, he was treated as a *captive*, *Shah Tahmasp* forced him to adopt the *Safavi religion*. (The *Safavid*, or *Sufi*, kings descended from a family of sainted dervishes, of the *Shiah sect*, who attained sovereignty, and established a scheme of religion called after their name; this became the religion of Persia.) Nevertheless—

1545—*Tahmasp* assisted *Humayun with 14,000 horse*. Humayun entered *Afghanistan*, wrested *Kandahar* from his brother *Mirza Askari*, whom he spared despite his officers. He then took *Kabul*, where *Hindal*, Baber's third son, joined him.

1548. *Kamran*, his third brother, who had rebelled [against him, now] joined him. (However, he was again subdued in *1551* after revolt; in *1553*, after fresh troubles, he was made prisoner, and had *his eyes put out*.)

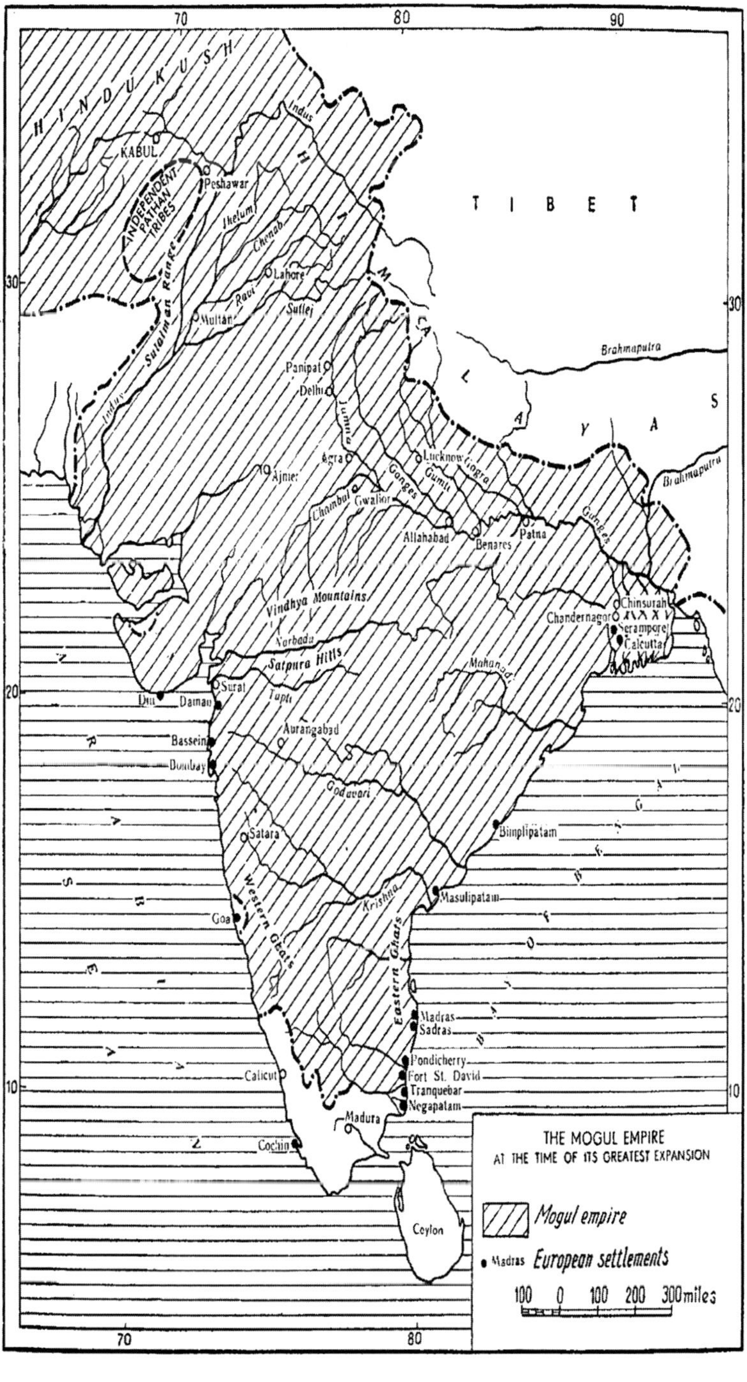

THE MOGUL EMPIRE
AT THE TIME OF ITS GREATEST EXPANSION

Humayun thus at the head of his family again; resided at *Kabul*.

Interregnum of the House of Sur at Delhi, 1540-1555

1540-1545. *Sher Shah at Delhi.*
1540. [He] took possession of the *Kingdom of Delhi* and renamed himself *Sher Shah* instead of *Sher Khan*; he seized all of Humayun's dominions.
1541. He conquered *Malwa*; in *1543*, [the fortress of] *Raisin*, and in *1544*, *Marwar*.
1545. He laid siege to *Chitor*; killed by chance shot from one of the town batteries. Succeeded by his *younger son*—
1545-1553—*Jalal Khan*; he became Shah of Delhi under name of *Selim Shah Sur*. Sher Shah's *eldest* son *Adil* sought to assert his rights, was defeated, and fled. *Fine public works under Selim Shah Sur.*
1553. *Selim Shah Sur* died, the throne was seized by his elder brother *Adil*.
1553-1554. *Muhammad Shah Sur Adil*; murdered his young nephew, Selim Shah's son; indulged in amusement; soon *outbreak of rebellion*, headed by one of his own family, *Ibrahim Sur*, who drove him off, and took *Delhi and Agra. Punjab, Bengal, and Malwa at once threw off all subjection.* Hearing of these disturbances—
1554—Humayun gathered army, and came from Kabul to claim his throne.
January 1555. *Humayun* set out from Kabul, invaded *Punjab*, took *Lahore*, *Delhi*, *Agra* without difficulty.
July 1555. *Humayun* restored to all his original grandeur.
January 1556. *Humayun killed* by accidental fall on some smooth marble; at that time *his son Akbar* (*13 years old*) was *in the Punjab* with his father's Minister, *Bahram Khan*; he was at once brought to Delhi by Bahram Khan.

(3) REIGN OF AKBAR, 1556-1605

1556. *At first Bahram Khan* was naturally the actual Governor; but while he was engaged in settling the home government at Delhi, *Mirza Suleiman*, *King of Badakh-*

shan, took *Kabul*, and simultaneously *Hemu*, Minister of Shah Adil, raised a rebellion.

Second Battle of Panipat. Hemu took *Agra*, Bahram went out to encounter him, both armies met at *Panipat*; *defeat of Hemu*, whom Bahram killed with his own hand; thus the family of *Sher Khan* done with.

Bahram returned to Delhi with a swelled head, had many persons, who presumed to oppose him, "done in.", in particular friends of *Akbar*'s too; so that—

1560—*Akbar took reins of government into his own hands*; *Bahram* went to *Nagar* in Rajputana, and as soon as Akbar had formally divested him of his office, he *revolted*. Akbar sent army against him, he was beaten, pardoned, but was killed by [son of] one of the nobles treacherously murdered by him. *Akbar* 18 years old; *his territory restricted to country round Delhi and Agra*, plus *Punjab*.

Almost immediately after acceding to the throne, he conquered *Ajmer*, *Gwalior*, and *Lucknow*; he then—

1561—*reconquered Malwa* from its rebellious Governor, *Abdullah Khan*, whom he sent into exile. That khan was an *Uzbek*, hence—

1564—his exile led to a *rising of the Uzbek tribe*, put down by *Akbar* in person in *1567*.

1566. *Hakim, Akbar's brother, seized Kabul*, of which he remained master for a long time.

1568-1570. *The Rajput States.*

1568. *Akbar* besieged *Chitor*; it fell after courageous resistance and death of its leader, killed by arrow. The surviving [nobles fled] to *Udaipur*, where their chief-
Hindu tain's family founded a new state and where *they* [continue] *to this day*. Thereafter *Akbar married two Rajput queens* in order to have peaceful connection with *Jaipur* and *Marwar*.

1570.[1] *Akbar* annexed *Rantambhor* and *Kalinjar*, two more Rajput [fortresses].

---

[1] 1569, according to Burgess, *The Chronology of Modern India*, Edinburgh, 1913.

1572-1573. *Gujarat.* Disturbances there (three groups, the strongest being *the Mirzas,*[1] descendants of Tamerlane, hence relatives of Akbar's; in *1566*, they had revolted in *Sambhal*, had been defeated, and had fled to Gujarat). Governor *Itimad Khan* insisted on Akbar's coming.

1573. Akbar [went] to Gujarat, *placed it under direct imperial rule*, beat the Mirzas, and returned to *Agra*. Fresh rebellion by the Mirzas; Akbar crushed them finally.

1575. *Bengal.* There *Prince Daud threw off dependence* (*no longer paid tribute*, etc.). Akbar [went] to Bengal, drove Daud to *Orissa*; as soon as he retired, Daud advanced again, regained his territory; Akbar defeated him in pitched battle, Daud killed fighting.

1575-1592. *Bihar*; ruled by *family of Sher Khan* since *1530*, re-annexed [by Akbar] in *1575*.—Shortly afterwards, rebellion among the imperial troops in Bihar and Bengal, not properly quelled during three years. Hence the *Afghans* expelled from Bihar seized the *Province of Orissa* and held it for some time.

1592. *The Afghans in Orissa finally crushed by one of Akbar's generals.*

1582. *Prince Hakim* invaded the *Punjab* from Kabul. Akbar drove him off, seized upon Kabul, pardoned his brother Hakim, made him Governor-General of the Kabul Province, *subject* to him as Emperor of Delhi.

1582-1585. Quiet; *Akbar settled the empire.* Was indifferent in religious matters, therefore tolerant; his chief religious and literary advisers were *Faizi* and *Abul Fazl.* Faizi translated old Sanskrit poems, including *Ramayana* and *Mahabharata* (later, after Akbar had brought a Roman-Catholic Portuguese priest from *Goa*, *Faizi* also translated the Evangelists. *Indulgence towards the Hindus*; Akbar only insisted on *abolition* of *suttee* (burning of widows on the husband's funeral pyre), etc. He *abolished jeziah*, i.e., *capitation tax*,

[1] Descendants and relations of Mirza (Prince) Muhammad Sultan, who came to India with Baber. They were Ulugh Mirza, Shah Mirza, and Ibrahim Husain Mirza, and they sought to seize the throne.

which every Hindu had been *compelled to pay to the Mussulman Government.*

Akbar's Revenue System (author, *Raja Todar Mall*, the Finance Minister); to *collect revenue from the cultivators*—

(1) First a uniform standard of measurement was established and then a *regular survey system* set on foot.

(2) *To ascertain the produce of each separate bigha*, and hence *the amount it ought to pay to the Government*, the land was divided *into three different classes, according to their varying degrees of fertility.* Then, for each *bigha*, the *average yield of its class was taken* and *the King's share made equal to one-third of this amount in kind.*

(3) *To settle the equivalent of this amount in money, regular statements of prices were taken over all the country for 19 years*, and the *average was the amount demanded in coin.*

The abuse of authority by petty officers was put down; *the amount of revenue* decreased, but the *expenses of collection lessened*, so that *net revenue* remained *same. Akbar abolished the custom of farming the revenues*, which had been *source of so much cruelty and extortion.*

Division of Empire into *15 provinces*; the chief officer in each called *Viceroy.*

Justice: *Kazi* represents the law, states the cases after full trial; *Mir-i-Adl* (Lord Chief Justice) represents the will of the Sovereign, *hearing the conclusion* and *passing sentence.* Akbar reformed the *Code of Punishments*, founding them partly on *Mohammedan custom*, *partly on the laws of Manu.*

Army: *Pay system in army* in great confusion; Akbar stopped abuses by *regular payment of the troops from the Treasury* and *keeping of lists of all the soldiers enrolled in each regiment.*

He made *Delhi* into the greatest and finest city then existing in the world.

1585-1587. Kashmir; in *1585*, disturbances in Kabul, occasioned by fear of *Uzbek* invasion; Akbar put them down by a great display of force.

1586. Failed in attack on *Kashmir*; in *1587*, *he succeeded*, and *annexed Kashmir.*

1587. *Peshawar and Neighbouring North-West Districts.* This country was held by the *Yusufzais*, a powerful Afghan tribe, belonging to the fanatic *Raushani* sect; they gave so much trouble to Kabul that Akbar sent two divisions against them, one under *Raja Bir Bal* and the other under *Zain Khan*. Both were all but annihilated; remnants of the imperial army fled to *Attock*. Akbar had these Afghans driven back into their mountains by sending another force; this was *the only success he ever attained over them.*

1591. *Sind*: invaded and *annexed* by Akbar on pretext of some internal troubles.

1594. *Kandahar* reconquered [by Akbar] from the *Persians*, who had retaken it on the death of Humayun. *Thus, in 1594, entire north of India under Mogul rule.*

Wars in the Deccan, 1596-1600

1596. *Attack by two armies* under *Prince Murad* (second son of Akbar) and *Mirza Khan* on *Ahmadnagar*, which was in the hands of the illustrious *Sultana Chand*; its siege and assault failed; Akbar was only allowed to annex *Berar*.

1597. New hostilities; *Akbar* reinforced through submission of the *Raja of Khandesh*, who joined his forces. Action by Murad on the Godavari River indecisive; *Akbar* joined his army on the Narbada.

1600. He sent his youngest son *Daniyal* ahead for the investment of Ahmadnagar, joined him then, *garrison murdered the gallant Sultana* and abandoned the city to the Moguls.

Selim's revolt brought Akbar back to Hindustan; during his father's absence, Selim had seized *Oudh* and *Bihar*; Akbar pardoned him, gave him *Bengal and Orissa*; cruel administration by Selim, Akbar about to go against him, Selim asked his forgiveness at Agra.

1605. The sudden death of his sons *Murad and Daniyal hastened Akbar's death* at age of 63. His only surviving son *Selim* assumed as Emperor the title of *Jahangir* ("conqueror of the world").

(4) REIGN OF JAHANGIR, 1605-1627

1605. At *Jahangir's accession to the throne*, Hindustan quiet, but disturbances in *Deccan* and a *war with Udaipur* proceeding. Jahangir kept all his father's chief officers in their posts; *restored the Mohammedan faith* as the established church; declared he would *maintain the law as before*. He *defeated and imprisoned* his son, Prince *Khusrau*, who during Jahangir's presence at Agra raised standard of revolt at Delhi and Lahore; impaled 700 of his followers on spikes and paraded Khusrau between the ghastly rows.

1610. Jahangir despatched two armies, one to the *Deccan*, the other to *Udaipur*. As regards the one sent to the Deccan, *Malik Amber*, Minister of the young *King of Ahmadnagar*, whose capital had been transferred to *Aurangabad*, had in 1610 recaptured *Ahmadnagar* (the Mogul garrison left there by Akbar defeated); not until—

1617—did the armies sent against *Malik Amber succeed in defeating* him, and that not in open fight, but solely through his allies' desertion.

1611. *Jahangir* married *Nur Jahan* (daughter of an emigrant from Persia), who dominated him completely, and plotted against his sons from earlier marriage.

1612. *Prince Khurram* (later *Shah Jahan*) conquered *Udaipur* and *reduced Marwar*.

1615. *Sir Thomas Roe*, first Englishman at court of Delhi, went there from *James I* on embassy concerning the embryo *East India Company*. *Jahangir* appointed *Khurram* (his third son) *successor* (the eldest, Khusrau, remained in prison, where he died in *1621;* and his second son, *Parviz*, he considered incompetent), made him *Viceroy of Gujarat* and sent him against *Malik Amber*, who had risen in arms again.

1621. *Nur Jahan* persuaded Jahangir to send Khurram (Shah Jahan) to Kandahar in order to remove him from Delhi and raise her favourite son Parviz to throne. Hence rebellious but futile attempts by *Shah Jahan*, who—

1624—reappeared in Delhi as a repentant sinner. Soon afterwards, *Mahabbat Khan*, sent against Shah Jahan, fell into disfavour with Nur Jahan, was recalled from the Deccan, and received cold treatment at Delhi. *Jahangir*, about to leave for Kabul, made *Mahabbat* accompany him, and treated him so harshly that Mahabbat took the opportunity, when all the imperial troops had crossed the *Hydaspes* (*Jhelum*, second of the five rivers of the Punjab from west to east), of seizing Jahangir and abducting him as captive to his own camp. *Nur Jahan* crossed the river, attacked Mahabbat at once, was defeated with heavy loss, whereupon she submitted, and joined Jahangir in his captivity. Mahabbat took the royal captives with him, treating them with distinction, while Nur Jahan recruited adherents in his army.

1627. On Nur Jahan's advice, Jahangir cantered away from the staff surrounding Mahabbat at grand review, and drawing near a unit entirely loyal to him, was *rescued by them*. Mahabbat was forgiven and *sent against Shah Jahan*, with whom, however, he fraternized at once.

October 28, 1627. *Jahangir* died on his way to Lahore. *Asaf Khan*, Governor of Delhi, sent at once for Shah Jahan, who arrived shortly after with Mahabbat Khan, and was solemnly crowned at Agra; *Nur Jahan* compelled to retire into private life.

(5) REIGN OF SHAH JAHAN, 1627-1658

1627.[1] *Khan Jahan Lodi's Revolt*. One of *Prince Parviz*'s generals, he joined the armies of the defunct Malik Amber's son; he then returned to Delhi on promise of pardon, but feeling distrustful, fled to *Chambal River*, engaged the royal troops there, was beaten, crossed the river, and fled through Bundelkhand to *Ahmadnagar*.

1629. *Shah Jahan* went in person to the *Deccan* against him; at *Burhanpur* he met him, and drove him back

[1] 1628, according to Burgess.

to *Ahmadnagar*; at *Bijapur*, *Khan Jahan* believed he would be safe under protection of his friend *Muhammad Adil Shah*, but the latter refused to admit him; he fled to *Malwa*, tried to force his way to *Bundelkhand*, but was defeated and slain. The Emperor then marched on Ahmadnagar.

1630[1]. While the latter was invested by the imperial army, *Fateh Khan* murdered the King of Ahmadnagar, whose Minister he was, and *surrendered the place to Shah Jahan*. Then the latter made fruitless attempt to take the city of *Bijapur*; he returned to Delhi, leaving *Mahabbat Khan* to besiege Bijapur and perform the duties of commander in the Deccan.

1634. After futile siege of Bijapur, Mahabbat Khan was recalled.

1635. *Bijapur* besieged by *Shan Jahan* himself—without success.

1636. *Shah Jahan*, therefore, made peace with *Muhammad Adil Shah*, King of Bijapur, and gave him the *territories of Ahmadnagar, which state thereby became extinct as independent sovereignty. Adil had foiled the entire Mogul army for six years.*

1637.[1] *Shah Jahan* [went] to Kabul; thence he sent army under *Ali Mardan Khan* (Governor of the new Mogul province of Kandahar, wrested from the *Persians* by Akbar in 1594) and his son Murad against Balkh.

1646. As both successful, *Balkh* was annexed and entrusted to *Aurangzeb*, third son of the Emperor.

1647. *Aurangzeb* besieged at Balkh by the *Uzbeks*; fled with great loss to India.

1648. *Persians under Shah Abbas retook Kandahar*; Aurangzeb sent to recover it; enemy cut his supplies off, he was forced to retire to Kabul.

1652. New attempt to recover Kandahar failed; ditto *1653*, when *Dara Shikoh*, the Emperor's eldest son, launched final attack on it. Moguls retired, *Kandahar Persian again*.

---

[1] 1631, according to Burgess.
[2] 1644, according to Elphinstone.

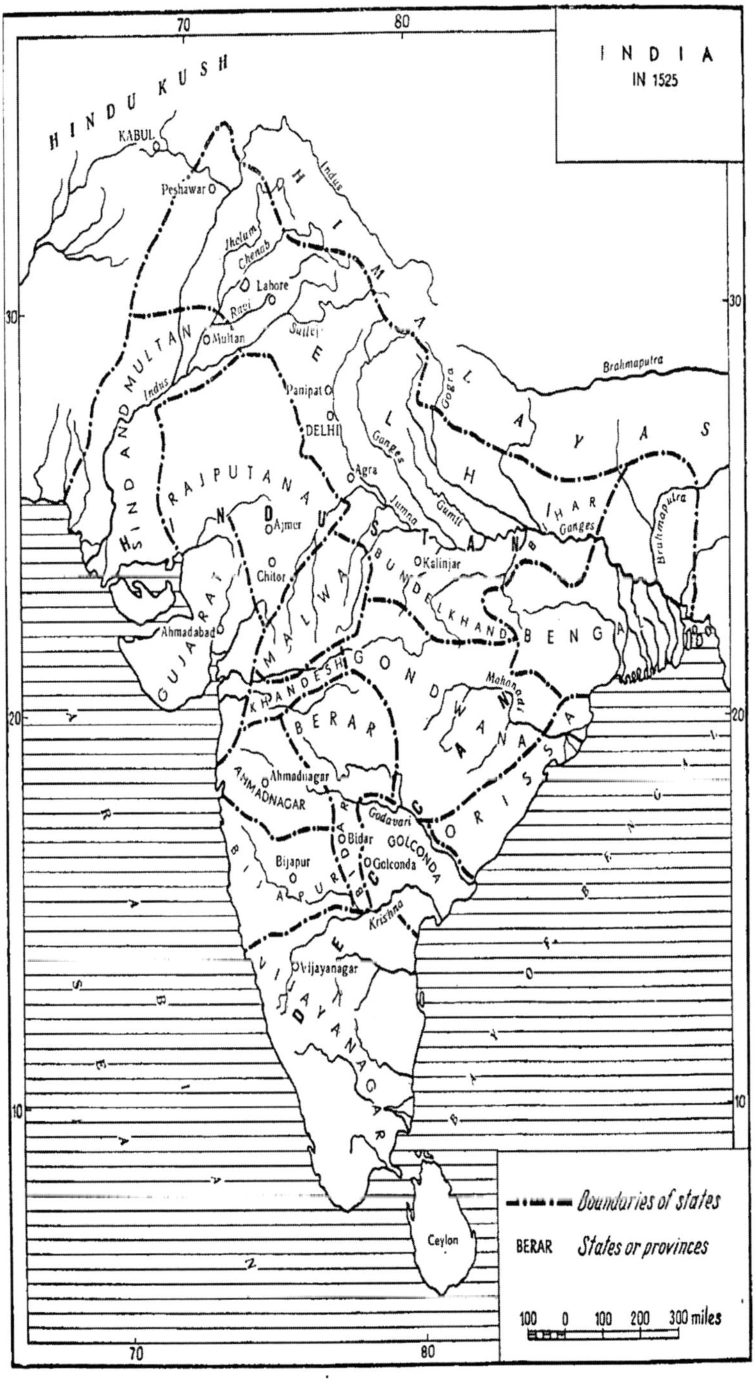
INDIA
IN 1525
HINDU KUSH
KABUL
Peshawar
Jhelum
Chenab
Lahore
Ravi
Multan
Sutlej
Indus
Panipat
DELHI
Agra
Jumna
Ganges
Gumti
Gogra
Brahmaputra
HIMALAYAS
MULTAN
SIND
RAJPUTANA
HINDUSTAN
Ajmer
Chitor
GUJARAT
Ahmadabad
MALWA
BUNDELKHAND
Kalinjar
BIHAR
BENGAL
KHANDESH
GONDWANA
Mahanadi
BERAR
ORISSA
Ahmadnagar
AHMADNAGAR
Godavari
BIDAR
Bidar
GOLCONDA
Golconda
Bijapur
BIJAPUR
Krishna
Vijayanagar
VIJAYANAGAR
ARABIAN SEA
BAY OF BENGAL
Ceylon
Boundaries of states
BERAR States or provinces
100 0 100 200 300 miles

1655. The Mogul armies back in the Deccan at application of *Mir Jumla*, Vizier of *Golconda*, threatened with death by his master, *Raja Abdullah Khan*. Thereupon *Aurangzeb* took possession of *Hyderabad* and—

1657—laid siege to *Golconda*; *Abdullah Khan* promised submission and *yearly tribute of £1,000,000*. Aurangzeb, on receiving word of *Shah Jahan's illness*, hurried back to Delhi. Shah Jahan had four sons: *Dara Shikoh*, *Shuja*, *Aurangzeb*, and *Murad*. *Dara* now Viceroy; *Shuja*, Governor of Bengal; *Murad* (the youngest), *Governor of Gujarat*. *Aurangzeb*, the third, calculating and cold, aspired to power and as he saw that *religion* was *the great motive power of the empire*, he sought popularity as *champion of Islam*.

Being taken ill, *Shah Jahan* entrusted government to *Dara*; *Shuja* revolted, marched on Bihar, ditto *Murad*, seized *Surat*. Aurangzeb let *Dara Shikoh* and *Shuja* weaken each other through struggle, and led his army to *Murad* on pretext that, while he wished to retire as monk from the world, he wanted first to help his youngest brother to the throne. *Shuja* was defeated by *Dara Shikoh*, who marched then on Murad and Aurangzeb, and was defeated.

1658. Contrary to *Shah Jahan*'s explicit wish, *Dara Shikoh* took the field again; armies met at *Samagarh*, near Agra; beaten thanks to Murad's courage, [Dara Shikoh] fled to his *father* at Agra; *Aurangzeb* went there, imprisoned both in a secure spot within the palace, treacherously seized *Murad* and jailed him at *Salimgarh*, a fort on the river opposite Delhi, removed him then chained to the *fortress of Gwalior*; *Aurangzeb* proclaimed himself Emperor in place of *Shah Jahan*, whom he had *dethroned*; he assumed the title of *Alamgir*.

(6) REIGN OF AURANGZEB, AND RISE OF THE MARATHAS, 1658-1707

1658. *Dara Shikoh* escaped from prison and fled to *Lahore* (where his son *Suleiman* tried to join him, but was intercepted and kept prisoner at *Srinagar*, capital of Kashmir). Dara then [proceeded] to Sind, while *Shuja* marched on Delhi and was defeated by Aurangzeb at *Khajwah* despite desertion, during the battle, of a *body of imperial troops under Raja Jaswant Singh,* who fled to *Jodhpur* after Shuja's defeat.

Presently Dara Shikoh took the field again [was defeated], fled to *Ahmadabad, Cutch, Kandahar,* and finally *Jun,* in Sind, whence he was treacherously delivered to Delhi and *executed; riot among the inhabitants of Delhi,* put down by force.

1660. *Prince Muhammad Sultan* (Aurangzeb's son) and *Mir Jumla,* the late Minister of Golconda, were successful against *Shuja in Bengal. Shuja* escaped to *Arakan,*[1] and no more was heard of him. *Muhammad Sultan* had revolted from Mir Jumla [and joined Shuja], then returned to duty. Aurangzeb *kept* him a *prisoner* for years until he died in gaol. The *Raja of Srinagar* delivered *Suleiman,* Dara Shikoh's son, as prisoner to Agra, where he *died* soon after, *poisoned by Aurangzeb.* Simultaneously *Murad* was murdered. From now on *Aurangzeb* was complete master of the situation (Shah Jahan still "under lock and key"). *Mir Jumla,* made Vizier, died at *Dacca* while on expedition against *Assam* [1663]; his place was taken by *Muhammad Amin,* his eldest son.

1660-1670. *Rise of the Marathas.*

One of *Malik Amber's officers,* namely, *Maloji Bhonslay,* had a son named *Shahji*; the latter married a daughter of *Jadu Rao,* an officer in high command; issue of this marriage, a son, named *Shivaji*; being always in contact with the rude soldiers of his father's *jagir* (tract of land given by the sovereign to an individual as a reward for special merit), he acquired habits of a robber, which he practised early in his retainers' company. He seized his father's own territory, captured many forts; he then began *open rebellion* by seizing a convoy of imperial treasure; his lieutenant took the *Governor of Konkan* prisoner, and occupied the whole province with its capital, *Kalyan.* After this success, *Shivaji* made overtures

[1] Old name of Burma.

to *Shah Jahan*, which were not received unfavourably. He then seized *South Konkan* and—

1655—went on extending his authority. *Aurangzeb* was sent to humble the pride of the Maratha. *Shivaji* plotted and cajoled, was forgiven; immediately after departure of the imperial force, he repeated his attacks on *Bijapur*. *Afzul Khan*, [commanding the troops] of Bijapur, agreed to have, unattended, private interview with *Shivaji*, who murdered him with his own hand, and then defeated the Khan's panic-stricken army.

After army had been sent against the now numerous bands of Shivaji's followers, the *new military commander of Bijapur*—

1660—went with force *against the Maratha country, defeated Shivaji*, and—

1662—made advantageous peace with him, leaving the rebel secured in a jagir in the Konkans.

1662. *Shivaji* began again to ravage Mogul territory. *Aurangzeb* sent against him *Shaista Khan*, who marched from *Aurangabad to Poona* and took it; he stayed there in winter quarters throughout the winter; one night Shivaji stole his way to him in order to murder him; Khan escaped, however. After the rains *Shaista Khan* went to *Aurangabad*, and *Shivaji* at once sacked *Surat*.

1664. *Shahji*, father of *Shivaji*, *died*, and in right of his father the latter became possessed of [Shahji's jagir] and [the territory near] *Madras*, as well as the *Konkans*, which he himself had conquered. He now assumed the title of *Raja of the Marathas*, and plundered the country far and wide.

1665. *Aurangzeb*, furious, sent army against him in two divisions. *Shivaji submitted*; still, under the *treaty*, this crafty man obtained another *jagir*, consisting of *12 out of the 32 forts he had captured, with their territory*. Besides, he obtained the *chauth*, a sort of *blackmail to be levied on all the Mogul land in the Deccan*, which afterwards [furnished] the Marathas [with] pretext for quarrelling with all the nations surrounding them and for encroaching on their territory.

1666. *Shivaji in Delhi as guest*; he was received so coldly (despite his "calculating," Aurangzeb did not assassinate him and in general behaved from the very beginning as an "ass" towards the Marathas) that he soon returned indignant to the Deccan. *In the same year, Shah Jahan died* in prison.

1667. *Through crafty intriguing, Shivaji* was *recognized under treaty as Raja*; he then overawed *Bijapur and Golconda*, and levied tribute on them.

1668 and 1669. *Shivaji settled his kingdom*; *made advantageous treaties with the Rajputs and other neighbours.*

1669. Thus the Marathas became a nation, governed by an independent sovereign.

1670. *Aurangzeb* violated the treaty; *Shivaji* first commenced operations by seizing *Poona*, and sacked *Surat* and *Khandesh*, while *Muazzam*, Aurangzeb's son, inactive at Aurangabad. *Mahabbat Khan* was despatched, and terribly beaten by Shivaji. *Aurangzeb recalled his armies and suspended hostilities. From then on, decline of Aurangzeb's influence*; all parties irritated against him; his *Mogul soldiers* furious over his futile Maratha campaigns, and the *Hindus, because he had re-introduced the jeziah and persecuted them on all sides.*

1678. *Finally he estranged the best warriors of his army, the Rajputs*, by his *conduct towards widow and children* of their great chief, *Raja Jaswant Singh*, who *died in 1678. Durga Das*, the Raja's son, plotted with *Prince Akbar*, Aurangzeb's son, marched on Delhi with *70,000 Rajputs.* The combination was broken by intrigue and defection, and the army disbanded before any action; *Akbar* and *Durga Das* fled to the *Marathas* under *Sambhaji*, son of the famous *Shivaji.*

1681. Peace in *Mewar* and *Marwar*, after the struggle between the two parties had gone on in desultory way. Meanwhile—

1673—*Shivaji* had seized the Konkans; in *1674*, he ravaged the *Mogul provinces of Khandesh and Berar*; idem *Shivaji*—

1677—captured one after another *Kurnul*, *Cuddapah* (he passed close to Madras, where the office-boys of *Eng-*

lish factories were in a blue funk—*May 1677, Madras records*), *Jinji*, and *Vellore*.

1678. Shivaji took *Mysore and Tanjore*, in *1680* he made a dash on *Bijapur*, cutting off the supplies of the Mogul army, and—

1680—*Shivaji* died on this expedition; his son *Sambhaji* took command of the Maratha forces. *Sambhaji* was a cruel and debauched prince; his power declined at once; had the Moguls had a good general, they would have broken Maratha power, but *Aurangzeb* continued like an "ox."

1683. *Sambhaji* defeated Prince *Muazzam*, who had been sent into the Konkans; the Marathas ravaged the country in the rear of the Mogul army, burnt the town of *Burhanpur*; thereupon *Muazzam* plundered Hyderabad and made treaty with *King of Golconda*, while the *Marathas*, marching northwards, sacked *Bharoch*.

Afterwards *Aurangzeb*, at head of another army, destroyed city and raj[1] of *Bijapur*, wantonly broke peace with *Golconda*, and captured that city.

From then on, *Aurangzeb* was *afraid of his own sons* and suspected everyone; his fear—

1687—became half madness; without any provocation he shut up his son *Muazzam* in prison, where the latter [spent] seven years.

Fall of the Mogul Empire dates *from that time*;

Deccan in confusion, *the native states were broken up*, country covered with bands of marauders; the *Marathas* were a great power; the *tribes of the North—Rajputs and Sikhs*—permanently alienated.

1689. A Mogul officer, *Tokarrab Khan* (*Governor of Kolhapur, near the Ghats*), hearing that *Sambhaji* was near by on hunting expedition, managed to seize him, sent him prisoner to *Aurangzeb*, who had him beheaded at once. *Saho* (*or Sahu*), *Sambhaji's* infant son, followed him, with the bold and prudent *Rajah Ram* as Regent.

1692. *Rajah Ram*, the Regent, reorganized the Maratha predatory bands, put the chieftains *Santaji* and *Da-*

[1] Kingdom.

naji in command, and sent them against the *Mogul armies* in a number of small engagements; that war lasted for about *five years*—1694-1699—of which three were occupied with *siege of Jinji*, finally occupied by the Marathas.

1694. *Aurangzeb* sent his general, *Zulfikar Khan*, to invest Jinji; the Khan asked for more troops, which were refused him; instead, *Prince Kambakhsh* was sent to take superior command; the Khan, hurt, spun out the siege; he held constant communications with the Marathas, and so, for three years, useless attempts by *Kambakhsh* to take the place.

1697. *Santaji* raised the siege; finally—

1698—as *Zulfikar Khan* realized that he would otherwise be disgraced by Aurangzeb, he *let the Maratha leader escape* and then stormed the fort without effort. Thereupon dissensions among the Marathas themselves; *Danaji* murdered *Santaji* with his own hand. *Hostilities resumed*; *Rajah Ram* himself headed a big army, and *Aurangzeb* on his part led the Moguls.

1700. *Aurangzeb* took *Satara* and till—

1704—*captured a great many Maratha fortresses. Rajah Ram died in the same year* [1700]. *Aurangzeb* now [1704] 86 years old. In the last four years of his life, whole government disorganized; *Marathas* began to recover their forts and gather strength; a terrible famine exhausted the provisions for the troops and drained the treasury; soldiers mutinous over want of pay; hard pressed by the Marathas, *Aurangzeb* retreated in great confusion to *Ahmadnagar*, fell ill, and—

February 21, 1707—*Aurangzeb* died at the age of 89 ("refused to let any of his sons approach his bedside").

[Penetration of European Merchants into India]

1497. In *December*, the Portuguese *Vasco da Gama* rounded *the Cape of Good Hope* and—

May 1498—cast anchor at *Calicut*. Thereafter *Portuguese colonies of merchants* were established at *Goa*, *Bombay*, and Point de Galle in *Ceylon*.

1595. (*A century later*) the *Dutch* obtained settlement near the present city of *Calcutta.*

1600. *London East India Company*—City Merchants Co.—[founded].

December 30, 1600, *charter* from Elizabeth *for trade* with the East in *silks, cottons,* and *precious stones.* The company to be managed by *"a governor and 24 committees".*

1601. Their first ships sailed [to India].—The *Great Mogul, Jahangir*—

1613[1]—granted those merchants a trading port at *Surat* by firman, and—

1615—allowed *Sir Thomas Roe to come on embassy to Delhi.*

1624. *The Company,* without any parliamentary interference whatever, *solicited* and *obtained* from *James I* the *authority* to *punish, by martial as well as by municipal law, their servants* [in India], hence, in fact, *"unlimited power over the lives and fortunes of the citizens"* (*James Mill*[2]). This was *the first judicial authority given by the Crown to the Company*; it extended only *over European British subjects.*

1634. *First factory established in Bengal by firman of Shah Jahan.*

1639. *The English allowed to trade at Madras.*

1654. The *Company's monopoly,* after 50 years' enjoyment of exclusive trade, imperilled by the formation of a new society, incorporated as *"The Merchants Adventurers."*

1661. To have no competition on Indian market, the *old Company* allowed the *"Adventurers"* to be *incorporated with them.*

1662. *Charles II wedded to the daughter of the King of Portugal; she brought as part of her dower the trading port of Bombay,* which thereby became *Crown possession,* but—

1668—*"the Merry* one" *presented the East India Co. with the port of Bombay. In this year,* the *first order for tea* (then called *tchay* after the Chinese) was sent from

---

[1] 1612, according to Burgess.
[2] Mill, *The History of British India,* Vol. I, London, 1858.

England to Madras. At the same time, *Charles II* gave them a *charter*, climax of monopoly doctrines, empowering the traders belonging to the *East India Co.* to *imprison and send to England any unlicensed person* whom they found there trading *on his own account*, etc.

1682. *The Court of Directors at home constituted Bengal into a separate presidency* (presidency meant then the *few factories and trading marts* scattered throughout a province), having a governor and council residing at *Calcutta*.

1688.[1] *Charnock*, the founder of Calcutta, was expelled from Bengal by the Moguls and, scared to death, fled up the river with the ousted merchants.

1690. The "dogs" returned from exile with Aurangzeb's permission; *Charnock now established permanent settlement in Calcutta, erecting forts and planting garrisons.*

1698. *Aurangzeb* allowed the "dogs," i. e., the "Company," to purchase the *three villages of Calcutta, Chutternutty*, and *Govindpur*, which were fortified afterwards. Sir *Charles Eyre* christened the *new fortifications Fort William* in honour of the "Dutch liberator"; *even now all public documents drawn up* are marked "*Fort William, Bengal.*"

In the same year, a new company was founded in England under *Charter of 9 and 10 William and Mary*; it gave power to any number of persons to combine and open commerce with East India *on a loan of £2,000,000, at 8%*; the subscribers allowed to trade, but *their exports not to exceed individually their separate shares of the loan*. Title of this company: *The English East India Company.*

1700. The new company all but flopped through costly and utterly useless embassy (to Aurangzeb) with Sir William Norris at the head.

1702. The "*old London Co.*" incorporated with the "*new one*"; from then on there existed only one, under title of *The United Company of Merchants Trading to East India.*

[1] 1687, according to Burgess.

In the same year,[1] *Aurangzeb* appointed one *Mir Jafar dewan* under title of *Murshid Kuli Khan.* (The *dewan* of a province was an officer of the Mogul Governor, who had to *superintend the collection of revenue and try all civil cases arising within the boundaries of his province.*) [Afterwards Jafar Khan] became *Subahdar of Bengal, Bihar, and Orissa.* (The *subahdar* was *viceroy* of a district; the two officers were often combined in one person.)
This gentleman hated les agréables Anglais,[2] interfered with their trade, and harassed them continuously. (In *1715*, they lodged a complaint against him with *Farrukhsher*, who gave the English merchants a *present of 38 towns*! and an *immunity from tax*, under a *dustuck*, or official pass, for each bale of goods, saving it from examination by the officials.)
Murshid Kuli Khan famous revenue officer; through unscrupulous systems of extortion and oppression, he created a large surplus out of the revenues of Bengal, *which was punctually remitted to Delhi.* He divided the province into *chaklas*, in every one of which *the chief collector* was an *officer, appointed by himself, who farmed the revenue. Afterwards these officers managed to constitute their posts hereditary*; *and claimed the title of "Zemindari Rajas."*

Aurangzeb was succeeded by *Prince Muazzam* as heir apparent.

(7) SUCCESSORS OF AURANGZEB TO THE GREAT BATTLE OF PANIPAT; EXTINCTION OF MOGUL SOVEREIGNTY, 1707-1761

(1) **1707-1712.** *Bahadur Shah* (this title was assumed by Muazzam).—*Prince Azim*, [Aurangzeb's] second surviving son, as well as Prince *Kambakhsh*, the third,

[1] 1704, according to Ramsbotham, *Studies in the Land Revenue History of Bengal*, Calcutta, 1926.
[2] The agreeable British.

rose in rebellion; they were both defeated and killed—each in the battle he fought with Muazzam. *Bahadur* rallied his energies against the *Marathas, fomented internal dissensions among their chiefs*, and finally *forced* an *unfavourable treaty* upon them.

1709. He made favourable treaties with the *Rajput states* of *Udaipur*, *Marwar*, and *Jaipur*.

1711. He *undertook expedition against the Sikhs, drove them from the Punjab into the hills.*—The *Sikhs* were religious body of deistical Hindus, arose in the *time of Akbar*; the "founder's" name was *Nanak*; formed into sect, directed by their *gurus* (spiritual chiefs), and remained quiet until the Mussulmans began to persecute them and in *1606* killed their leader. Then they became fanatical haters of everything Mohammedan; they formed military power under famous *Guru Govind*, and overran the Punjab.

1712. *Bahadur died* at 71 years of age, and after much fighting and many murders was succeeded by his half-witted son—

(2) **1712-1713**—*Jehandar Shah*; he made *Zulfikar Khan* his Minister; raised slaves to the posts formerly held by nobles. *His nephew Farrukhsher*—

1713—revolted in Bengal, defeated imperial army near Agra, and put Jehandar Shah and Zulfikar Khan to death.

(3) **1713-1719.** *Farrukhsher*. His two chief accomplices among the nobles, *Sayyid Abdullah* and *Sayyid Husain*, forced him to grant them high posts at the court; he was secretly afraid of them. *Husain* went to Deccan, where the *Governor*, *Daud*, secretly instigated by the Emperor, opposed him, but was killed at the time of victory. *Husain* then [went to war] against the Marathas, failed to achieve anything, and finally made peace with the young *Raja Sahu*, which peace Farrukhsher refused to recognize, considering it disgraceful.

1715. (See p. 56.[1]) The *English businessmen of Calcutta* sent deputation to Delhi against the *Viceroy, Murshid*

[1] P. 49 of this edition.

Kuli Khan; one of the delegates was surgeon Hamilton, who cured the Great Mogul of a disease, hence, *etc.*, *see p. 56*.

1719. *Husain*, called from the Deccan by the "threatened" Sayyid *Abdullah*, assassinated Farrukhsher in the seraglio with his own hand. During the first two months after his death, the rebel nobles raised and deposed two minor princes, and finally fixed upon a prince of the royal blood, namely, *Mohammed Shah.*

(4) **1719-1748.** *Mohammed Shah.* Several revolts broke out at once.

1720. *Asaf Jah, Governor of Malwa*, proclaimed himself independent.

(His real name: *Chin Kilich Khan*, son of a *Turki* noble, *Ghazi-uddin*, a favourite officer of Aurangzeb's; he became Governor, first of the Deccan, then of Malwa; also called *Nizam-ul-Mulk*, and his descendants became *Nizams of the Deccan.*) He defeated, at *Burhanpur* and *Balapur*, the imperial troops, commanded by the *Sayyids*; the Great Mogul, fearful of these, made *Asaf Jah* his Vizier soon after, but later felt him to be a nuisance, and—

1723[1]—[*Asaf Jah*] retired to the *Deccan.—Sayyid Husain* murdered by a Kalmuck (under orders from the Emperor, it appears); (Sayyid) *Abdullah* tried to set up a new emperor, was defeated and imprisoned.—*At that time the Rajputs wrested Gujarat from the empire.*

1725. *Mohammed Shah* instigated Mubariz, *Governor of Hyderabad*, to go against Asaf Jah; the latter beat and killed him, and sent his head to Delhi.

1720. *Death of Balaji Viswanath*, who as *Raja Sahu*'s Minister had consolidated the latter's empire. He was the *first "Peshwa,"* title borne by the Minister of the Maratha Raja. (*Later the peshwas seized all real power, while the royal family lived quietly at Satara*, losing importance and becoming in time *merely "rajas of Satara."*) He was succeeded by his energetic son *Baji*

[1] 1724, according to Elphinstone.

Rao (*the greatest of the peshwas and the ablest Maratha save Shivaji*); he advised Sahu to strike at the Mogul Empire itself. Sahu left him all power. *Baji Rao* ravaged Malwa.

1722.[1] *Baji Rao* attacked *Asaf Jah* (then Governor of the Mogul) at *Hyderabad*; defeated him signally.—In addition, he ravaged *Gujarat*.
The leaders of the Maratha armies at that period were the founders of the *three great Deccan families*: *Udaji Puar*, Malhar *Holkar*, and Ranaji *Sindhia*.

1733.[2] *Secret pact between Baji Rao* and *Asaf Jah* on mutual support.

1734. *Malwa and Bundelkhand captured by the Marathas.* The Emperor ceded them the conquered districts and gave them a right to levy *chauth on Asaf Jah's dominions*; this broke up the alliance [between Asaf Jah and Baji Rao], and *Asaf* returned to his allegiance.

1737. *Baji Rao* ravaged the country beyond Jumna and appeared suddenly before *Delhi*, but retired without attacking. *Asaf Jah* marched against him, was defeated near [Fort] *Bhopal* and *compelled to cede whole country between the Narbada and the Chambal to the Marathas. Thereby the Marathas established themselves in the North.*

1739-1740. *India invaded by Nadir Shah.* (He was originally a *freebooter*; had with a few followers joined the exiled Shah of Persia, *Tahmasp*, when the latter was expelled by the Khiljies. Nadir helped *Tahmasp* to regain the crown, then pushed him aside and made himself Shah. He reduced Kandahar and Kabul, and then invaded India.)

1739. *Nadir Shah* took Lahore, and defeated Mohammed Shah at Karnal. The Emperor submitted, and accompanied Nadir to Delhi. Hindus murdered many Persians in Delhi, whereupon *wholesale massacre of Hindus*; Nadir's rapacity and violence.

1740. *Nadir, loaded with treasures,* [returned] *home*, and left the *Mogul Empire tottering to its fall.* In the *same*

[1] 1727, according to Elphinstone.
[2] 1731, according to Burgess.

year, the Marathas resumed offensive, *Peshwa Baji Rao died*, and was succeeded by his son *Balaji Rao*.

1743. *Balaji Rao* marched on *Malwa*, and renewed his demands on the Court of Delhi; Emperor *gave him Malwa*, belonging to *Raguji Khan*, who had revolted.

1744. *Balaji* beat Raguji, drove him off, and then retired to *Satara*.

1744.[1] *First invasion of Ahmad Khan Durani. Nadir Shah murdered*; the *Afghan tribe of Abdali*, or *Durani* (as it was called afterwards), under *Ahmad Khan seized the Punjab*; he was beaten by Mohammed's son *Ahmad Shah*.

1748. *Asaf Jah* died, ditto *Mohammed Shah*; succeeded by his son *Ahmad Shah*.

1749. *Raja Sahu died*; *Balaji* placed on throne *Rajah Ram*, grandson of *Rajah Ram the elder* and his wife *Tara Bai*.

(5) **1748-1754.** *Ahmad Shah*. He soon had quarrels with the *Rohillas*, who were Afghans of [the vicinity of] Oudh. (The *Rohillas*, Afghan tribe, emigrated from *Kabul*—apparently first to the north-west Himalayas, named Rohilla Himalayas—settled in the *late 17th century* in the north-eastern part of Delhi, between *the Gogra and the Ganges*, in what they named Rohilkhand.) He was unable to cope with them; they forced their way into Allahabad, and the Vizier, *Safdar Jang*, called in the Marathas to help him against them; the Marathas repelled [the Rohillas], and in recognition of their help the *Maratha leaders, Sindhia and Holkar*, were *rewarded with jagirs*.

1753.[2] *Second invasion of the Punjab by Ahmad Khan Durani*; quietly ceded to him. He assumed the title of *Shah*.

1754. *Ghazi-uddin*—[son of] *Asaf Jah*'s eldest son—with whom the Great Mogul had had quarrel, seized him, put out his eyes, deposed him, and proclaimed one of the princes of royal blood [Emperor] under the title of—

---

[1] 1748, according to Elphinstone.

[2] 1751, according to Elphinstone.

(6) **1754-1759**—*Alamgir II* (Aurangzeb called himself Alamgir I), making himself the latter's Minister; *Ghazi-uddin governed execrably*, several attempts by the people to murder him; this very same Vizier—

1756—treacherously seized a son of [the Governor of the Punjab, appointed by] *Ahmad Shah Durani*, who came to Delhi, sacked it, and when he returned to *Lahore*—

1757—*Ghazi called in the Marathas, and with their aid retook Delhi.*

1758. *Raghoba*, the Maratha leader, took the Punjab from Ahmad Shah Durani, and conspired with Ghazi-uddin to bring *all Hindustan* under Maratha rule.

1759. *Ghazi-uddin* murdered *Alamgir II*, the last Great Mogul with any real power.

1760. *Sadasheo Bhao*, a Maratha chieftain, then commanding the armies of the Peshwa (having made extensive preparations for the conquest of Delhi and then marched northwards), *took Delhi*. At once the *Afghan* [Rohilla] *leaders* under command of *Ahmad Shah Durani* crossed the Jumna at the height of the rainy season, while *Sadasheo Bhao* took up strong position *at Panipat*; there the two gigantic armies of invaders, each bent on the conquest of the capital of India, confronted each other.

January 6, 1761. *Third Battle of Panipat.* On that day the Maratha leaders informed *Sadasheo Bhao* that he must *offer battle* at once or the Marathas would disperse. (Until then, the two armies had confronted each other in fortified camps, constantly harassing each other and cutting off supplies; the Marathas suffered severely from starvation and disease). Sadasheo marched out; *furious battle*; the Marathas had all but won the day when Ahmad Shah Durani ordered *his own centre* to charge, and at the same time had his left flank by-pass the Marathas' right flank and attack it. This movement [proved] decisive. The Marathas fled in disorder, their army almost annihilated; they (appear to have) left some 200,000 dead on battlefield, and the remnants of their troops fell back over the Narbada.—*Ahmad Shah*'s army, too, was so shattered in the contest that he retired to the Punjab without reaping the fruits of his victory.

Delhi was *deserted*; there was no one to govern it; the governments all around were shattered; *Marathas never recovered from the blow.*

State of the Country after the Battle at Panipat:

Mogul Empire gone; the *nominal Emperor, Ali Gohar,* wandering in *Bihar.*—The *Peshwa* of the Marathas, *Balaji Rao*, died of grief; his power was divided among the four great chieftains: the *Gaekwar* in *Gujarat*; the *Raja of Nagpur* (Bhonslay), *Holkar*, and *Sindhia. The Nizam* at *Hyderabad* became independent sovereign, but his power crippled through losses and weakened by the French policy of protection towards him.

In *1761, the year of the Battle of Panipat, the English had ousted the Frenchmen from southern India; on January* 16, 1761, the French abandoned *Pondicherry invested by Coote*, who had its fort pulled down; thus *every vestige of French power in India* was *destroyed. The Nabob of* the *Carnatic* was completely dependent on good will of the *English Governor of Madras*; the *Nabob of Oudh had become independent, with large territories and fine army*; the *Rajputs* splendid soldiers, but scattered; *a united Rajput sovereignty* unheard of; the *Jats and Rohillas* became powers of some consequence, and later played prominent role in Indian history.—*Haidar Ali*, with whom the English soon in contact, was great authority in *Mysore.*—The *English* were already then probably greatest force in India. They *had appointed the crowns of two large possessions —the Subahdari of Bengal, Bihar, and Orissa*, and the *Nabobship of the Carnatic*; soon after, their ally, *Nizam Ali*, imprisoned his brother, the *Subahdar of the Deccan*, and seized his throne, placing *all of southern India under British influence.* (See p. 68.)[1]
(Continued, p. 84.)[2]

. . . .

[1] The passage in question appears on pp. 97-101.

[2] Here Marx gives, following his chronological notes, an abstract of Kovalevsky's book, whose chapters he entitles: (D) The Process of Feu-

[A Survey of Foreign Invasions of India]

331 B. C. *Darius Codamanus* finally defeated by *Alexander Magnus* in *Battle of Arbela*, near the mountains of Kurdistan.

327 B.C. *Alexander* reduced *Afghanistan*, then crossed *Indus* into territory called *Taxila*; its chief concluded alliance with Alexander against the great Raja *Porus*, or *Puru*, reigning in *Kanauj over all Hindustan*.

326 B.C. Alexander opposed by Porus on the *eastern bank* of the *Jhelum*, or *Hydaspes*; Hindus defeated in pitched battle; but Alexander's army would not advance farther into India; hence Alexander took his whole force on board of a vast number of galleys and sailed down the Hydaspes to the Indus; he reached—after severe fighting on the route—the *mouth of the Indus* and divided his army into two parts, *one division, under Nearchus*, having orders to sail up the Persian Gulf, while *Alexander* himself returned *by land* with the other. This was the *last invasion of India before the Mohammedans came*[1].

Of the *old kingdoms of Hindustan*, *Kingdom of Bengal* destroyed in *1203 A. D.* by the Mohammedans (*Ghur Dynasty, Shehabuddin*), under the reign of the 6th, or *Sena, Dynasty*.

1231. *Kingdom of Malwa* destroyed by Mohammedans (by *Shamsuddin Altamsh, one of the slave kings of Delhi*).

1297. *Kingdom of Gujarat* destroyed by the Mohammedans (*by Ala-uddin Khilji*); its kings were Rajputs; according to legend, the kingdom was founded by *Krishna*.

1193. *Kingdom of Kanauj* (very rich in 1017, when Mahmud of Ghazni seized its capital) was destroyed and its capital sacked (by the brother of *Ghiyasuddin*—

---

dalization of Agriculture in India under Mussulman Rule (pp. 62-67); (E) British Domination and Its Effect on Indian Communal Property (pp. 68-76). After these two chapters comes an abstract of the two closing chapters of Kovalevsky's book on Algeria. The chronological notes are continued on p. 84 of Marx's note-book.

[1] This assertion is borrowed from Elphinstone, who apparently knew nothing about the invasions of India bythe Yuchi, Sacae, Huns, and other tribes between the 4th century B. C. and the 7th century A. D.

Ghur Dynasty—Shehab). The reigning prince, *Shivaj*, fled to *Jodhpur* in Marwar and established a Rajput state, now *one of the wealthiest.*

1050. *Principality of Delhi*, then very insignificant, conquered by *Visal, King of Ajmer.*

1192. *Kingdom of Ajmer*, insignificant, and *Delhi*, which was *dependent* on it, overthrown by the Mussulmans (under *Ghiyasuddin*, Ghur Dynasty). The old states—*Mewar, Jaisalmer, and Jaipur*—still in existence; the *Mewar family oldest in India.*

1205. *Sind* fell into Mussulman hands, being conquered by *Shehabuddin Ghuri*. (In *325* [B.C.], in the days of Alexander Magnus, independent state; afterwards divided and again reunited; in *711*, invaded by Mohammedans, who were beaten back by the Rajput leader at head of the *Sumera tribe.*)

1015. *Kashmir* fell into *Mahmud of Ghazni's* hands.

(*Kingdom of Magadha* was a most interesting one. Its *Buddhist kings* wielded extensive power; they belonged for many years to the *Kshatriya caste*, until one of the *Sudra* caste—the fourth and lowest of Manu's four castes—named *Chandragupta*—called Sandracottus by the Greeks—murdered the King and made himself sovereign; he lived in *Alexander Magnus*' time. Later we find *three more Sudra dynasties*, which ended with one *Andhra* in *436 A.D*. One of the *kings of Malwa* was *Vikramaditya*; the Hindu calendar still bears the date of his era; he reigned in 58 B. C.)

. . . .

Old Deccan States. There are five languages in the *Deccan*: (1) *Tamil*, spoken in the *Dravira* land, i.e., the *extreme south*, bounded by line running through Bangalore, along the Ghats to Coimbatore and Calicut; (2) *Kanarese*, a dialect of Telugu, in *North and South Kanara*; (3) *Telugu*, spoken in *Mysore* and the countries to the north; (4) *Marathi*, written in the *Devanagari alphabet* and having the following limits: *north*, the *Satpura Hills*; *south*, the *Telugu country*, called Telingana; *east* River *Wardha*; *west*, *the hills*; (5) *Oriya, a rough dialect spoken in Orissa*. Between Orissa and the Maratha country are the *Gonds*, who speak a rough jargon.

The *Ramayana* glorifies the exploits of *Rama, King of Oudh*; he is supposed to have lived about *1400* B.C.; according to the poem, he was the Hindus' conquering leader in the march on *Deccan* and *Ceylon*; in the course of that legendary *invasion*, the Hindus found in Deccan many *civilized nations*: *Tamils* speaking the *Tamil language*, and others in the *Telinga country*, whose vernacular was *Telugu*. The *most ancient kingdoms were the Tamil.*

About 5th century, B. C., *Pandya* was founded by a *shepherd king of that name*; small country; capital, the ancient town of *Madura*, and territory, the *present* districts of *Madura* and *Tinnevelly* in the extreme south of the Carnatic; remained independent till *1736 A. D.*, when conquered by *Nabob of Arcot.*

Chola, where *Tamil* language spoken; capital was *Conjeeveram*; in *1678*, a *Maratha* chieftain, *Venkoji*, supplanted the King, and became the *first of the present rajas of Tanjore.*

Chera was a little state including *Travancore*, *Coimbatore*, and *part of Malabar.*

Kerala, *colonized by Brahmins of Hindustan*, governed by an aristocracy of that caste; included *Malabar* and *Kanara*; by and by split up into factions, and went to pieces; *Malabar* became possession of the *Zamorins* (*rajas of Calicut*), while *Kanara* was seized by the *rajas of Vijayanagar.*

Carnata, mentioned in earliest accounts [as divided] between the princes of *Pandya* and *Chera*. It had one great and powerful family, the *Belala Rajas*, overthrown by the Mohammedans in *1310* (under *Ala-uddin* Khilji).

The *Yadavas* mentioned, their locality obscure, nothing known of them.

The *Chalukyas of Carnata*, a Rajput family living at *Kalyan*, to the *west of Bidar*; another branch of the same family—

The *Chalukyas of Calinga*—ruled over tract in *East Telingana*, extending along the coast up to the *borders of Orissa*; they were overthrown by the rajas of Cuttack.

Andhra, capital was *Warangal*; *several dynasties* (one of which, the *Ganapati Rajas*, attained great eminence), ruled for more than 400 years, and in *1332* were *overthrown* by the Mohammedans (*under Muhammad Tughlak*).

Orissa: first notice of this raj, in *Mahabharata*; the earliest authentic date, *473 A. D.* (expulsion of the invading "yavanas"[1] by the ruling family). *Thirty-five "Kesari" Rajas* succeeded each other until, in *1131*, the *dynasty overthrown by that of Ganga Vansa*, which family on throne till *1550*, when country seized by Mohammedans (under *Selim Shah Sur--Jalal Khan, see p. 49*).[2]

Lastly, Greek author of *Periplus* mentions two great cities as important trading marts on the coast, named *Tagara* and *Plithana*; nothing known of them, their site supposed somewhere near the *Godavari River*. For the "ancient" in Hindustan, cf. also *Hastinapuram* (the petty state concerning which the war [described] in the Indian *Iliad, Mahabharata*, was waged); the ancient religious city, *Muttra* and *Panchala* (p. 6).[3]

---

[1] At that time all foreigners in India were called *yavanas*. It is not clear who are meant in this particular case. The first authentic date is that of the reduction of Orissa by Asoka, who ruled approximately from 270 to 232 B. C.

[2] See pp. 33 of this edition.

[3] This and subsequent references by Marx are to the pages of Robert Sewell, *The Analytical History of India*, London, 1870.

[THE CONQUEST OF INDIA BY THE BRITISH EAST INDIA COMPANY]

I. THE EAST INDIA CO. IN BENGAL, 1725-1755

(*Great Moguls*: *Mohammed Shah, 1719-1748*; *Ahmad Shah, 1748-1754.*)

1725. *Death of Murshid Kuli Khan, Subahdar of Bengal, Bihar, and Orissa* and *Dewan* (collector of revenue) for Bengal; succeeded in the *Bengal and Orissa* appointments by his son Shuja-uddin.

1726. Trading on the *Hooghly* were: the *English, at Calcutta*; *French, at Chandernagor*; *Dutch, at Chinsurah*, and the *Ostend East India Co.*, established by German Emperor, had founded [a factory] at the *village of Banki Zabar*; the other companies rallied and threw the *interlopers*[1] out of Bengal. In the same year (under George I), *Mayor's courts* were set up in each *presidency town*; see p. 79 for more about this extension of *English common and statute law* to India—quoad[2] English.

1730. In England a new society, formed on free trade principles, begged *charter from Parliament* for *East India trade*; simultaneously the *old East India Co.* asked for prolongation of their *monopoly charter*, as their *period of incorporation* had expired by then; hard parliamentary battles, the old monopoly company won; *their charter prolonged till 1766.*

---

[1] Merchants who traded with India on their own, thereby violating the East India Co.'s monopoly.

[2] Concerning.

1740.[1] Subahdar *Shuja-uddin* died, and was succeeded by *Aliverdi Khan*, Governor of Bihar, who thus *reunited* the three provinces of *Bengal, Bihar*, and *Orissa*; he was—

1741—attacked by the Marathas, who plundered factory at *Murshidabad*, etc. (pp. 79, 80). As a result the English—

1742—obtained from *Aliverdi Khan* permission to dig the celebrated *Maratha Ditch*.

1751. Marathas, bought off by Aliverdi Khan, retired to Deccan. From then on, the *British settlements on the Hooghly enjoyed peace till 1755* (cf. pp. 79-80 for the Maratha affair)

. . . .

II. WAR WITH THE FRENCH IN THE CARNATIC, 1744-1760

1744. *Great war declared* in Europe *between England and France*; the *English troops in Madras Presidency only 600*; the *French troops, under Labourdonnais*, more numerous at Pondicherry and Ile de France.[2]

September 20, 1746. *Labourdonnais captured Madras*; he neither imprisoned *the English merchants*, nor injured them personally; this enraged his *rival Dupleix*, the Governor of *Pondicherry*. (This fellow was son of a *French East Indian Director*); in *1730*, Governor of a large French factory at *Chandernagor*, on the *Hooghly*; was made Governor of Pondicherry in *1742*. *His rivalry against Labourdonnais* ended in the downfall of French in India.

The *fleet under the command of Labourdonnais* having been destroyed by a storm, Dupleix sent him no assistance. Labourdonnais *taken prisoner by the English*. Returning to France, he died *in Bastille in 1749*. (In *1735*, he had been sent as *Governor* to Ile de France and Bourbon[3] and in *1741*, his term having expired,

[1] 1739, according to Burgess.
[2] Old name of Mauritius.
[3] Old name of Réunion.

was sent out in *command of an expedition of nine vessels to damage the trade of the English in India*; on the declaration of war in *1744*, he sailed to take the command of the French in the South.)

1746. *State of Parties in the Deccan.* Under Great Mogul *Mohammed Shah* (*1719-1748*) was *Asaf Jah*, alias *Nizam-ul-Mulk, Subahdar of the Deccan*, who founded the *Dynasty of the Nizams*, and resided at *Hyderabad.* Thanks to him, *Anwaruddin* became *Nabob of the Carnatic* in 1740, at the *death* of its *minorennis*[1] hereditary Nabob, whose guardian the same Asaf Jah had appointed him earlier. By marriage with the *daughter of Dost Ali*, former Nabob of the Carnatic, *Chandar Sahib* had become *Governor* of *Trichinopoly*, whence he was ousted by the Marathas in *1741*, and fled to the French at Madras.

1746. *Anwaruddin* (Nabob of the Carnatic) with 10,000 men attacked *Madras*, where *Dupleix* was at head of the French; the Nabob pushed back by about 1,000 Frenchmen under Dupleix, who ravaged town, burned several [English] factories, and sent the more prominent English inhabitants to Pondicherry.

December 19, Dupleix attacked *Fort St. David*, 12 miles south of Madras (where English had a garrison of 200), with 1,700 men, but Anwaruddin marched against the besieging French and forced them to *retreat to Pondicherry.*

1747. Dupleix won Anwaruddin to his side; he attacked *Fort St. David* again in *March*, [but] retired at approach of *English fleet* under *Captain Peyton*, who left reinforcements.

June **1747.** *Admirals Boscawen and Griffin* arrived from England at Madras with fleet, thereby increasing *British force in the South to* 4,000; English invested Pondicherry, [but] retreated empty-handed.

October 4, 1748. *Word received of the Peace of Aachen*; Dupleix had restored Madras to the English.—*Sahuji*, Maratha Prince at *Tanjore*, fifth in descent from *Shahji* (father

[1] Juvenile

of *Shivaji*), whose *jagir* was [Tanjore], invoked English support against his younger brother *Pratap Singh*, who had wrested power from him and the [centre] of whose rebellion was the stronghold of Devikota, in the mouth of the Coleroon.

1747.[1] Sahuji promised the *English* to *cede* them that stronghold if they took it. *Major Lawrence*, with *Clive* serving under him as young officer, took it; thus Devikota became English. But *Pratap Singh*, for his part, finally forced *Sahuji* to abdicate on promise of annuity of Rs 50,000.

1748. *Death of Nizam-ul-Mulk, Subahdar of the Deccan*; he was succeeded by his son *Nazir Jang*, whose title was disputed by the son of a defunct elder brother, *Muzaffar Jang*. A war broke out between the two.

1749. *New war between English and French. Muzaffar Jang* turned to *French* for help and obtained it, as well as the alliance of *Chandar Sahib*, whom he promised to make *Nabob of Arcot* if he assisted him to the subahdari.—On the other hand, *Nazir Jang* (*the Nizam*) had the *English* and *Anwaruddin* (Nabob of the Carnatic) for allies.—*Anwaruddin* was killed in first skirmish, and his troops fled to *Trichinopoly*; but mutiny broke out over pay in the French army, which left Dupleix in the lurch; Nazir Jang advanced, Muzaffar Jang was defeated and captured, while *Chandar Sahib* desperately fought his way to Pondicherry. After the victory Nazir Jang entertained himself in Arcot. English retreated to Madras.

1750. *Mohammed Ali*, son of Anwaruddin, succeeded him as *Nabob of the Carnatic*; this fellow, secured in his office by English, remained their willing servant, hence his sobriquet, "*the Company's Nabob.*"—*Dupleix* victoriously launched the campaign of that year by capturing the *fortresses* of *Jinji*, *Masulipatam* and *Trivadi*, and defeating Mohammed Ali. Incited by him, some traitors, *Pathan nabobs*, in the Nizam's (Nazir Jang's) camp finished him [the Nizam] off; the latter was succeeded by his nephew *Muzaffar Jang*

[1] 1749 according to Burgess.

(ally of the French), *Subahdar* in his own right. He made *Dupleix Nabob of the Carnatic and Chandar Sahib, Nabob of Arcot*; but—

January 4, 1751—while journeying with large retinue in the State of *Hyderabad, Muzaffar Jang* was killed by the same Pathan nabobs who had finished off *Nazir Jang*. Muzaffar Jang had no direct issue; next heirs apparent were *Nazir Jang's sons*; *Bussy*, who was in command of the French contingent, conferred the vacant post [of subahdar] on *Salabat Jang*, Nazir Jang's youngest son, held as prisoner in the camp at the time of Muzaffar Jang's murder.

Meanwhile Chandar Sahib, marching from Arcot, attacked his former seat of government, *Trichinopoly*, but Captain *Clive* countered him by marching on *Arcot*, which he took, and forcing him into a hasty retreat. After *seven weeks' fruitless besieging of Arcot*, Chandar Sahib returned to *Trichinopoly*, whither—

1752—*Clive* followed him; he stayed there with Mohammed Ali and Major Lawrence; *Chandar Sahib*, fugitive, was treacherously finished off by the *Raja of Tanjore*, an English protégé.

1753. The English ally, *Mohammed Ali*, had promised *Trichinopoly* to the *Raja of Mysore*, but was unable to keep his word, for the place was now held by the English. *Dupleix* took advantage of this to [make] an alliance with the *Raja of Mysore* and, through him, with the *Marathas under Morari Rao*.

May 1753-October 1754. Dupleix with his allies invested *Trichinopoly*, successfully held under *Lawrence and Clive*.

In the *same year* (under George II), the *Mayor's courts*, which had fallen into disuse since the capture of Madras by Labourdonnais in 1746, were re-established in *Madras*. They acquired jurisdiction in *all matters between Europeans*, as well as *between Hindus*, but only on their consent, *expressly exempting those who refused to be subject* to this tribunal. "*This charter is the first instance we find of the reservation of their own laws to the people of India.*" (Grady's *Hindu Law of Inheritance*, Introduction, p. XLIV.)

1754. *Peace; recall of Dupleix* (this was *signal of the downfall of the French in India*). For there had been dispute in Europe since *1751* as to who should be recognized as *Nabob of the Carnatic: Mohammed Ali, "the Company's Nabob,"* or *Dupleix*, officially *appointed by the hereditary Subahdar*; but English Government contended that it should be Mohammed Ali as heir to the former Nabob and because none but the phantom Great Mogul *Ahmad Shah* (d. 1754; succeeded by *Alamgir II, 1754-1759*), *could by express firman transfer the office from the hereditary line.* Dupleix' enemies in France plotted against him "because of the heavy expenses" he had incurred. *Dupleix* superseded by *Godeheu* (1754). (Dupleix died a few years later in dire poverty in France! The *envy* of those French poodles is the undoing of able men.)

December 26, 1754. *Peace treaty signed between Godeheu* and *Sanders* (Governor of Madras), whereby *Mohammed Ali was recognized as Nabob of the Carnatic.*—Meanwhile *Bussy*, the cleverest of all French leaders in India, [was] in *Aurangabad* with *Salabat Jang*, the Deccan Nizam, assisting him in managing the affairs of the subahdari.—In the same year—*1754*[1]—Salabat Jang was attacked by *Ghazi-uddin Khan* (elder brother of the former Subahdar, Nazir Jang) at head of a large army, joined by the *Marathas.* Bussy beat the latter and had *Ghazi-uddin poisoned*; the Nizam thanked him by giving the *Northern Circars*[2] *to the French.*

1755. *Contrary to Bussy's advice, Salabat Jang* attacked the *Raja of Mysore*, who had refused to pay him tribute (the Raja of Mysore, then *French* ally, was thereby urged into alliance with English); expedition successful; Raja of Mysore bought off Salabat Jang with large sums of money and presents. The Nizam then joined *with the Marathas under the Peshwa, Balaji Rao*, and defeated the rebel Maratha chieftain, Morari Rao.

---

[1] 1752, according to Elphinstone.

[2] Province in the north of the Coromandel Coast; it belonged to the Nizam of Hyderabad.

1749-1756. *Maratha Affairs.* In 1749, *Raja Sahu* died at *Poona* without issue; *Balaji Rao*, the *Peshwa*, became the real ruler; [he] left the remaining prince of the blood. *Rajah Ram*, nothing but title keeping him virtually as prisoner. At the same time he sent his bold and refractory son—*Raghoba*—away from *Poona*, on pretext of plundering the dominions of the *Gaekwar of Gujarat*.

1756. *Bussy*, ordered by the Nizam, Salabat Jang, away from his court, went to *Masulipatam*; he heard that the Nizam proposed to ally himself with the English in order to expel the French from the subahdari. He at once took offensive and entrenched himself at *Charmal*, near *Hyderabad*. Salabat came of terms, and declined the English alliance.

1757. The *Nizam* again sent Bussy away to the *Northern Circars.* But soon he had to recall him: on his return—

1757—*Bussy* found four *opposing armies* collected round Hyderabad, under the *Nizam's* two *elder brothers*, viz., *Basalat Jang* and *Nizam Ali*, with the latter of whom, moreover, *Salabat Jang's* Minister conspired; Bussy had him *slain* in an apparently accidental struggle; thereupon *Nizam Ali* fled from the battlefield, while *Basalat Jang* was bought off by presenting him with the fortress of *Daulatabad*.

1758. *Bussy* now dictator of the entire Deccan; *just then* the enviously dull-witted *rabble of Louis XV removed him*, replaced him by the *Irish* adventurer *Lally*, good soldier but no general.

May 1, 1758. *Lally* landed near *Fort St. David* and at once ordered Bussy to march south with all the French under his command; Bussy obeyed; Lally took *Fort St. David*, and was about to attack *Madras*; the *French merchants* at Pondicherry *refused him the smallest pecuniary assistance*; he therefore decided to "loot" *Tanjore*, reputed to be very rich, and besieged it closely; Raja of Tanjore appealed to the *English*; these sent fleet from Madras to *Karikal*, cut off the French supplies, and landed an army that proceeded to *draw lines round the parallels of Lally's attack.* French siege raised, and the *French Admiral*, in direct contradiction to orders, *sailed with fleet to Mauritius, leaving Lally to his fate.*—Lally took *Arcot*, was joined there by *Bussy*; the latter advised him to *remain* at *Arcot* in order to consolidate French power and collect funds for the final descent on the English headquarters; but the "crazy" Lally insisted on his plan and—

December 12, 1758—*invested Madras*, where garrison, commanded by *Lawrence*, held out for two months; on *December* 14, *French* captured "*Black Town*" and drew parallels round the fort.

February 16, 1759. A *British fleet* appeared in the roads, siege raised; Lally fled, leaving 50 guns behind him *Colonel Coote*, who had come with the fleet, landed unhampered at Madras, marched out with the garrison, captured Wandiwash, and shattered *Lally*, driving him to *Pondicherry*.

1760. *Lally at Pondicherry*, waiting in vain for supplies from France; his troops mutinous for pay; at *end of 1760*, Coote began *siege* of Pondicherry.

January 14, 1761. Garrison evacuated Pondicherry; *Coote razed the fort to the ground, completely destroying every vestige of French power in India. Lally was terribly maltreated and at last executed in Paris*; *Labourdonnais* died in gaol, *Dupleix* in misery, *Bussy* stayed in India until forgotten.

. . . .

III. EVENTS IN BENGAL, 1755-1773

1740, when *Aliverdi Khan*, following death of the Subahdar, Shuja-uddin, united the three provinces of *Bengal, Bihar, and Orissa* under himself (p. 85[1]), saw the *death of Baji Rao*, the *Maratha Peshwa*. (His armies were led by *Puar, Holkar, Sindhia*, and a powerful adventurer, *Raghoji Bhonslay*.) With his death *Raghoji Bhonslay's* power became so great that the other leaders entered private contract to crush him; [they] had him *sent on an expedition to the Carnatic*. The *Pesh-*

[1] P. 61 of this edition.

wa (*Baji Rao*) left three sons: *Balaji Rao*, who succeeded him, *Raghunath Rao* (later famed as *Raghoba*), and *Shamsher Bahadur*, who was ruling in *Bundelkhand*. The *grants of land* which the new Peshwa, *Balaji Rao*, received brought him into *direct* opposition to *Bhonslay*, who thereupon invaded *Bengal*, but was defeated by the royal troops. *Aliverdi Khan* was compelled by these hostile occurrences in his own country to *defend himself* against the Marathas of both parties; he was reinforced with *imperial troops*; *Bhaskar*, an officer of *Balaji Rao's*, opposed him successfully, fought him as far as *Katwa*, advanced to the *Hooghly*, and plundered a *factory at Murshidabad*.

In *1744*, *Bhaskar* assassinated by Aliverdi Khan, who in *1751* bought off the Marathas.

1755. English made alliance with *Balaji Rao*, the *Peshwa*, in view of his growing might and the weakness of the Great Mogul.

April 8, 1756. *Aliverdi Khan died*; succeeded as *Subahdar* by his grandson *Suraj-ud-daula*; [he] at once sent message to *Mr. Drake*, Governor of Calcutta, to *raze all the British fortifications*. On Drake's refusal he came down on Calcutta in force. As the fort garrison only 120 English artillerymen, etc., and no supplies in the fort, Drake gave the inhabitants the order of "sauve qui peut."[1]

Evening, June 21, 1756. The clerks, etc., decamped; in the night, fort defended by *Holwell* "by the light of the burning factories," fort stormed, garrison taken prisoners, *Suraj gave orders* that *all the captives should be kept in safety till the morning*; but the *146 men* (accidentally, it seems) were crushed into a room 20 feet square and with but one small window; *next morning* (*as Holwell himself* tells the story), only 23 were still alive; they were *allowed to sail down the Hooghly*. It was "the *Black Hole of Calcutta*," over which the *English hypocrites* have been making so much sham scandal to this day. *Suraj-ud-daula* returned to *Murshida-*

[1] Save himself who can.

bad; Bengal now completely and effectually cleared of the English intruders.

January 2, 1757. *Fort William* recaptured by *Clive*, sent up from Madras with *fleet under Admiral Watson.* Subahdar marched on Calcutta, attacked by Clive, *in decisive action* of many hours. On *January 3, Suraj-ud-daula restored the Company to their old privileges and* [paid them] *compensation.*—*Clive* destroyed French settlement at *Chandernagor*. Subahdar fixed his camp at *Plassey* (on *Hooghly*, near Calcutta). *Mir Jafar*, Commander-in-Chief of the Mogul army, *wrote letter to Clive*, offering to *desert* to English on any day of general engagement if he were made *Subahdar* of Bengal, Bihar, and Orissa in place of *Suraj-ud-daula*. Clive accepted offer.

June 23, 1757. *Battle of Plassey*. Entire Mogul army defeated, Subahdar fled, *Mir Jafar* ceased fighting, [deserted] to Clive's camp.

June 29, 1757. [English] army returned to *Murshidabad*, where Clive solemnly *made* the traitor *Subahdar of Bengal, Bihar, and Orissa* on condition that he would pay the war expenses and *protect the Company's possessions* on the *Hooghly*; *Dulub Ram* became Mir Jafar's *Minister of Finance* and *Ram Narayan, Governor of Patna.*

June 30, a son of Mir Jafar found Suraj-ud-daula disguised as a mendicant, and *finished him off.*

Immediately after Battle of Plassey, Clive made *Governor of Calcutta*; thus he was now *British civil and military commander in Bengal.*

Three revolts against Mir Jafar—in Midnapore, Purnea and Bihar—put down.

End of 1757. Arrival of a treasure-ship with £ 800,000 from Mir Jafar; it delighted the Calcutta "dunderheads."

1758. *Colonel Forde*, sent on an expedition by Clive, defeated the French under Conflans in *Vizagapatam*, and captured *Masulipatam.*

1759. *Ali Gohar*, the *Shah Zada* (Prince Imperial), eldest son of the Great Mogul *Alamgir II*, revolted against his father, was joined by Subahdar of Oudh, and marched on *Patna*, defended by *Ram Narayan*; *Clive* came to the latter's assistance, put the Shah Zada to flight, and received from Mir Jafar a *jagir* bringing £ 30,000 a year.—Shortly after, a *Dutch fleet* [coming] from their settlements in *Batavia* appeared on the Hooghly, and landed some troops; in the *night*, Clive had *Colonel Forde attack* them and throw them back into their boats; the *Dutch commander* withdrew after promising to pay all expenses.

February 25, 1760. *Clive sailed for Europe.—Dulub Ram*, Mir Jafar's Minister of Finance, *assassinated* by the latter.—Meanwhile the Great Mogul, *Alamgir II*, was likewise murdered—by his Vizier, *Ghazi-uddin*; *Shah Zada* proclaimed himself Emperor, marched on *Patna*, and defeated Ram Narayan, who held out in the city till—

February 20, 1760, when Colonel *Caillaud*, arriving with British force, defeated the new Emperor (*Ali Gohar*); the Mogul undertook flanking march on *Murshidabad*, found English drawn up there, and retired to *Patna*. Caillaud sent Captain Knox to relieve that city; Knox advanced with 200 Europeans, battalion of sepoys, and a small squadron of cavalry. *Knox* beat Moguls and fixed his camp at Patna, but *Nabob of Purnea* appeared on *other bank of the Ganges* with 30,000 men and more than 100 cannons.

May 20, 1760. *Victory of Knox*, who, supported by his ally, *Rajput Raja Shitab Roy*, crossed river for the *offensive*; Mogul army put to flight; Knox and the Rajput entered Patna with only 300 survivors.

January 6, 1761. *Battle of Panipat* (cf. p. 58[1]) between the *Marathas* under *Sadasheo Bhao* and the Durani, or *Abdali* (*Afghan* tribe), *under Ahmad Khan Abdali*. Mogul Empire in India utterly defeated; Maratha strength shattered and *Ahmad Khan* weakened to such an extent that he had to return to Afghanistan.

1757. *Raghoba* (called in by Alamgir II's Vizier, Ghazi-uddin) took *Delhi* from Ahmad Khan; after defeating *Prince Timur*, Ahmad Khan's son, *in the Punjab*, the

[1] Pp. 54-55 of this edition.

Marathas returned to the *Deccan*. On return to *Poona*, *Raghoba* quarrelled with *Sadashiv* (or *Sadasheo*) *Bhao*, *the Peshwa's cousin*, and was removed from the army command, Sadasheo being put in his place.

1759. *Ahmad Khan* invaded India for the fourth time and took *Lahore* just when *Ghazi-uddin* had murdered *Alamgir II* and when *Najib-ud-daula*, an *Afghan* commander, had driven the *Maratha leaders*, *Malhar Rao Holkar* and *Dataji Sindhia*, across the Ganges. Thereupon—

Early 1760—*Ahmad Khan* [appeared] with *army before Delhi*. *Bhao* (*Sadasheo*) marched against him with immense army, and there *was final decision at Panipat*.

1760. *Vansittart, Governor of Bengal in place of Clive*; as a *Madras civilian* he was "disliked" by the Bengalese *officers*. — *Vansittart* removed *Mir Jafar* and made his son-in-law *Mir Kasim* Subahdar; this fellow lived in *Calcutta* scrupulously paying the English his subsidy of £200,000; *ceded absolutely to the Company one-third of his territory*, viz., the *districts of Midnapore*, *Burdwan*, and *Chittagong*. But afterwards, irritated at the interference of Vansittart, he began increasing and disciplining his army.—Meanwhile *Ali Gohar*, under title of *Emperor Shah Alam*, unable to regain Delhi, *ravaged Bihar*, finally made *alliance with the English*, was recognized by them at *Patna*, and confirmed all the appointments they had made.

1762. *Mir Kasim* imprisoned *Ram Narayan*, had his collectors torture the *ryots*, etc., but his sin as the *Company* saw it was this: the asinine Great Mogul, *Farrukhsher* (see p. 56.[1]), had in 1715 guaranteed the *Company as a collective body* the *dustuck* (immunity of tax for imported commodities); but all *private traders* (English) had grasped this loan as their right. *Mir Kasim* was against this usurpation by "clerks"; his *collectors* sought to carry out his orders, *seized goods which had not paid duty*, and were insulted by the *Company's servants*. *Vansittart* promised privately that Mir Kasim

[1] P. 49 of this edition.

should be paid a *duty of* 9% [by the Company's servants]; *Council of the Company* quashed that, and issued *formal order to seize and imprison Mir Kasim's officers* if attempting to enforce the duty. *Mir Kasim* countered by *granting a firman to all Mogul traders at the port that they should pass their goods free of duty*; thereby he put them on *even. terms* with the English "clerks."—*Ellis*, chief of *the English factory at Patna*, began openly to prepare for war. Two fellows, *Hay and Amyatt*, sent *from Calcutta to Monghyr* to insist on the Company's claims, were seized on *orders from Mir Kasim*; *Hay* was held as hostage for the good behaviour of Ellis, *Amyatt* sent back to Calcutta with written remonstration from Mir Kasim.—*Ellis* at once *seized city and fort of Patna*. Mir Kasim ordered his officers to seize every Englishman who came their way; on his way to Calcutta *Amyatt*, loath to surrender his sword to *Mogul police, fired on them*, and was himself killed in the scuffle.

1763. *Mir Kasim* increased his army, and applied for help to the Great Mogul (Ali Gohar) and the *Subahdar of Oudh*; the English declared him deposed, reappointing *Mir Jafar* in his place.

July 19, 1763. English victorious (it was *opening of the campaign*), ditto July *24*; on *August* 2, after taking *Murshidabad*, the English victorious at *Gheria*; *Mir Kasim finished off all his English prisoners*, including the *Setts, the great Murshidabad bankers*, and also murdered Ram Narayan.

November 1763. English took Mir Kasim's camp at *Udwanullah*, the Mogul [Mir Kasim] fled to *Patna*, was there joined by the Great Mogul, *Shah Alam*, and the *Subahdar of Oudh* with large force; but *English took Patna by assault.*

1764. In Patna, because of pay arrears, *the sepoys revolted* against the English; the sepoys marched out of the city to join enemy; they were attacked and defeated by *Major Munro*, and marched back to *Patna*, where the *ringleaders were blown from the guns* (so this philanthropic operation was *employed* as early as *that first sepoy uprising*!).

October 22, 1764. *Mir Kasim,* attacked by Munro in his *fortified camp at Buxar,* was defeated, and fled for his life to *Oudh.*

1764. Through this *victory at Buxar* (north-west of Patna), *entire Ganges bank* [fell] into English hands, the English becoming *virtual masters of Hindustan.* Vansittart at once recognized *Shuja-ud-daula as Nabob of Oudh; Mir Jafar,* as *Nabob of Bengal, Bihar, and Orissa* (*Mir Jafar* had *to pay subsidy of* 53 *lakhs*); *Shah Alam,* as Great Mogul, with residence at *Allahabad.*

1765. *Mir Jafar* died; his son *Najm-ud-daula* recognized as his successor.—Vansittart's term of office expired *in the same year; Clive, made peer,* became his successor; in the *interim, Spencer* appointed President [of the Calcutta Council of the Company].

Clive's Second Administration, 1765-1767. (Clive quarrelled in London with the *Directors of the East India Co.,* who at once sent orders to Calcutta to stop the rent-payment of his jagir.)

May 3, 1765. *Lord Clive landed at Calcutta,* vested with combined powers of *Governor of Bengal, President of Council, and Commander-in-Chief.*

Corruption, which Clive found in Calcutta, etc. (p. 103). The *Committee of Four,* appointed to assist Clive, were *General Carnac, Mr. Verelst, Mr. Sumner, and Mr. Sykes.—Clive* induced the *Nabob of Bengal, Orissa, and Bihar,* the debaucher *Najm-ud-daula,* to abdicate for *annual income of 53 lakhs of rupees,* transferring over all *his powers to the East India Co.;* he also gave the *Great Mogul* annuity of *26 lakhs of rupees* for the *free cession of all territorial rights in those three districts,* and secured the revenues of *Kora* and Allahabad; furthermore, Great Mogul ceded *all jurisdiction* over the newly acquired country *to the East India Co.* Thus English Government acquired *Dewani*[1] and *Nizamat.*[2] In the same year, Clive made the *Adalat System*[3] constitutional (see pp. 104, 105). The *East India*

---

[1] Department of Finance.
[2] War Department.
[3] Government through native administration.

Co. thereby acquired *absolute government over 25 million people*, and an *annual revenue of 4 crores of rupees.* (It was not until *1772* that *Warren Hastings was authorized to place the entire administration in the hands of English officers.*)

January 1, 1766. *Clive ordered* that *double batta should cease* from *that day* (the extra pay called "batta" was received by the English officers when employed in the field; it had been *doubled* during the recent war). Thereupon *mutiny of the Bengal officers;* together they sent in their resignations, something which seemed all the more unfortunate as just then came news of advance of *50,000 Marathas on Bihar*. Clive accepted all the resignations, sent the offenders to court-martial, and ordered up in their place all the *cadets and officers* from *Madras.* The *British troops, desirous of following* the example of their officers, were *held in check by the faithful sepoys*! Sir *Robert Fletcher*, Commander-in-Chief at Calcutta, was *dismissed* without more ado, rightly or wrongly, as conniving in the conspiracy.

Inland Trade Disputes. The *Directors of the East India Co. had* [in the absence of Clive] allowed *their servants to monopolize the inland trade in salt and areca-nuts*, whole service rushed into speculation, skinning ryots; *discontent of the natives.* Clive put an end (!?) to it, instituting a *society for the promotion of inland trade* yielding the Company a steady profit, but preventing individual speculation at the expense of the natives; two years later, the society was liquidated on direction from the board at home and replaced by *a regular commission.*

1767. *Resignation of Lord Clive* on account of illness. On *his return to England*, he was cruelly persecuted by the Directors of the Company.

November 1774, suicide of Clive!

1767-1769. *Verelst*, President [of the Council] at Calcutta, Governor of Bengal; *1772-1785, Warren Hastings.* Was a *Bengal civilian*, born in *1732*, in *1750* sent to Calcutta *as clerk*. In *1760*, member of Calcutta Council.

1769. *300,000 Marathas* sent northwards by *Peshwa Madhu Rao* to avenge the defeat at Panipat; [they] ravaged Rajputana, forced the Jats to pay tribute, and advanced on *Delhi*, well governed by *Zabita Khan*, son of *Najib-ud-daula* the Rohilla, left there by Ahmad Khan in 1756; they [the Marathas] offered *Shah Alam* to reinstate him in triumph at *Delhi* if he placed himself exclusively under Maratha protection. He accepted.

December 25, 1771. The fellow [Shah Alam] was crowned *Mogul Emperor* at *Delhi* by the Peshwa.

1772. Marathas overran Rohilkhand, reduced the *Doab*, laid waste the whole province; they imprisoned *Zabita Khan* and confiscated his property.

Autumn 1772. [Marathas] made treaty with the Rohillas and the *Nabob Vizier of Oudh*, Shuja-ud-daula; *retired* on his promise to pay *40 lakhs of rupees*, which he did not keep.

1773. *Marathas* determined to plunder Oudh; the *Rohillas under Hafiz Rahmat* allied themselves against them with the *Nabob of Oudh*. The witless *Shah Alam* attacked the *Marathas*, was thoroughly worsted; victors forced him to cede the *districts of Kora and Allahabad*; but those districts included part of the *British territory of Bengal*. The British "brutes" were in luck, for the *Peshwa at Poona* recalled all the *Marathas to Deccan* for expedition to the south.

Events in England. Envy there over the immense fortunes of the Company's servants; besides, the luxurious way of life of the fellows. *Source of this wealth, wholesale depositions of native princes, disgraceful system of oppression and extortion*, denounced, like the entire system of the Company, in *Parliament*. The rules under which a *holder of £500 stock* had one vote at the meetings of the *Court of Proprietors* had led to system of extensive bribery and corruption in the *annual election of new Directors*. On one occasion, Lord Shelbourne spent £100,000 merely to have Mr. Sullivan elected to the Directorate. The *India House* was a constant scene of intrigues and jobbery.

1771. Parliament interfered, appointed a *Committee of Three* to go to Calcutta to examine the whole machinery of the Company and make reforms. The three—*Providence!* —viz., *Vansittart*, *Scrafton*, and *Colonel Forde*, lost their lives in *shipwreck off Cape of Good Hope*.

Soon afterwards, *dispute between East India Co. and British Government* over the *actual ownership of the English possessions in India.*

During these discussions, revealed: *temporary bankruptcy of the Company*; deficit to a million pounds *in India* and $1^1/_2$ millions in England. The Directors begged permission of Parliament to contract a *public loan*; *death-blow to the illusions about the inexhaustible wealth of India*!

1772, *select committee appointed*; the whole *system* of fraud, *violence, oppression, by which certain individual members had enriched themselves, laid bare.* Impassioned debate in Parliament; *Lord Clive's* celebrated speech on Indian affairs.

1773. *Reconstruction Act* [on the East India Co.] passed through both houses; *amount of stock* qualifying for one vote—no proprietor might have at *Court of Proprietors more than four* votes—raised from £500 to £1,000. *Governor of Calcutta* was renamed "*Governor-General,*" *having supreme command over all the presidencies* and *nominated by Parliament every five years. New constitution of courts* (pp. 109, 110).—Under Warren Hastings' partially adopted plan (in *1780, the Governor-General in Council* received from *Parliament power* to make rules and regulations for the newly acquired countries; at that time the 23d rule of *Warren Hastings* made law nem. con. The 27th section exacted that the *Koran* should be the standard of law for Mohammedans; the *Vedas* or *Dharma Shastras,* for Hindus), the natives were *to have their own laws* administered to them; by 23d rule of Warren Hastings, *maulavies* (expounders of the Mohammedan law) and *pundits* (interpreters of the Hindu law) were appointed to attend regularly in each court.

. . . .

IV. AFFAIRS IN MADRAS AND BOMBAY, 1761-1770

1761. *Salabat Jang, Subahdar of the Deccan,* seized and imprisoned by his brother *Nizam Ali,* who proclaimed himself Nizam.—The *President of Madras* demanded from

Mohammed Ali, "the Company's Nabob" (of the Carnatic), 50 lakhs of rupees for the maintenance of the "*English contingent*" of troops guaranteed to him; Mohammed told them [the English] to fleece *Tanjore*; President of Madras threatened the Raja of Tanjore with "confiscation" of his dominions unless he paid the money; the latter consented; *in this manner the expense of the Carnatic contingent was defrayed!*

1763. "*Peace of Paris*" recognized *Mohammed Ali* as *Nabob of the Carnatic* and *Salabat Jang*, as *Subahdar of the Deccan*. Thereupon the latter was finished off by *his brother Nizam Ali*, who, now *Subahdar*, declared war on English, and refused to recognize Mohammed Ali as Nabob of the Carnatic. A few English regiments frightened him into quietude. Simultaneously *firman* was received from the *puppet Emperor at Delhi*, declaring the Company's ally, the *Nabob of the Carnatic, independent of the present or any future subahdar of the Deccan*. Thus *Carnatic* became an *independent sovereignty*.

August 12, 1765. *Clive* persuaded the puppet Emperor to give up the *Northern Circars to the English*; the *Nizam* refused to recognize this [deal], and sent threatening message to the *President of Madras*, saying that *these lands* (which true) *had been given to the French*; President of Madras sent *Colonel Caillaud* to Hyderabad where—

November 12, 1766—*first treaty with the Nizam* [*was concluded*]; by its terms, *Northern Circars* to be held by the *English from the Nizam*; Company had to pay him *annual subsidy* of 8 lakhs of rupees and to detail 2 battalions of infantry with 6 guns to defend the district.

1761. *Haidar Ali became Raja of Mysore*, took *Bednore* in *1763* and *South Kanara* in *1764*.

Haidar Ali born *1702*; *son of Fateh Mohammed*, a *Mogul officer*, who died in command of small troop in the Punjab, leaving his son as *naik* (was in Mogul army= capitaine in French army; nowadays, in the native army, a *corporal* is called naik) with 200 men under his orders. Haidar Ali, with his 200 men, joined *army of*

Mysore in *1750*. At that time the *Raja of Mysore* had resigned all power to his Vizier, *Nanjaraj*. In *1755*, Haidar Ali was made commander of the *fortress of Dindigul*, with order to raise body of troops and maintain them; he did so by marauding and inviting *all criminals and freebooters* in the neighbourhood *into his fortress*; they flocked to him in large numbers. Thus in *1757*, when *Peshwa invaded Mysore*, *Haidar* had force of 10,000 men, many guns, and ammunition. He *received large estate by way of reward*. Mysore treasury, exhausted by payments to buy off the Marathas, was depleted, and hence mutinies of the unpaid soldiers, which *Haidar* had greatly helped to quell. In *1759*, Haidar was made *Commander-in-Chief in Mysore*, received *more land* as present, thus becoming *possessor* of *half the raj* in his own right; *Nanjaraj*, overawed, resigned, and *Haidar* became *responsible minister* of the Raja; he was attacked by *Khande Rao*, induced Nanjaraj to reassume the viziership pro hunc,[1] went to the army, defeated and captured *Khannde Rao*, whom he—a second *Louis XI*—shut up in an *iron cage* like a paroquet, had him fed on *crumbs of rice and seeds*, in mockery; the bird soon died as a result, and then, in *1761*, *Haidar* forced *Nanjaraj and the Raja to resign in his favour*.

1765. *Peshwa Madhu Rao* sent army against Haidar Ali under *Raghoji Bhonslay* (then *Raja of Berar*) and the Peshwa's brother *Raghoba*. Twice defeated, *Haidar* bought off the Marathas with 32 lakhs of rupees and by *cession of all the territories* he had conquered beyond the Mysore frontier.

1766. *Haidar Ali* reassumed offensive, and captured *Calicut* and *Malabar*. *Peshwa* made great alliance with the *Nizam* and *English* against Haidar.

1767. *First Mysore War*. In *January 1767*, Peshwa crossed Kistna, and his Marathas plundered northern Mysore; by large payment Haidar induced him to withdraw his troops to *Poona*.—Nizam joined Haidar (see *Treachery of the Nizam against Nanjaraj*, p. 114). Thus the English

[1] For the time being.

under *Colonel Smith* had to retire. In *September 1767*, *Smith* was attacked by the united armies of Mysore and Hyderabad at *Chengama* (in *South Arcot, Madras Presidency*); he defeated them and withdrew in excellent order to Madras.

1768. *Demonstration by the English* against place near *Hyderabad*; Nizam, cowed, came to terms.

Second (English) treaty with Nizam (exceedingly blameworthy and most *characteristic of the East India Co.!*). By its terms, the English to *"pay tribute" to Nizam for the Northern Circars*. The *"Guntur Circars,"* then held by the Nizam's brother *Basalat Jang*, not to be claimed by the Company until after the latter's death. The English to pay *chauth* (blackmail) *to the Marathas* (was paid them only by the surrounding little states in order to buy off encroachments by those marauders, as of old among the *Highland tribes of Scotland*!). To *be able to pay this chauth*—voilà le couronnement de l'œuvre[1]—*the English pledged themselves to conquer the Carnatic Balaghat from Haidar Ali* and *pay the chauth out of the proceeds* of that annexation!

Autumn 1768. *Expedition from Bombay* conquered *Mangalore* and *Onore*; reconquered from the English by *Haidar* one or two months later. But while he was thus engaged on western coast, *Colonel Smith* marched into *Mysore* from the east, took almost half of it, and *laid siege to Bangalore*. The *Mysoreans* drove him back all the way to Kolar.

1769. At *Kolar*, for many months, English did nothing; meanwhile *Haidar* ravaged the Carnatic, Trichinopoly, Madura, and Tinnevelly; *by the end of 1769*, Haidar had regained all his territory and reinforced his army. *Colonel Smith* marched into Mysore against him, but Haidar eluded him by *flanking march*, appearing suddenly *before Madras. Panic among the "office-boys."*

1769. They made *offensive and defensive treaty with Haidar*, and *Colonel Smith*, on their orders, was compelled to let Haidar march unmolested past his camp and back into Mysore.

---

[1] This is what crowns the work.

1770. *Haidar Ali* now turned against Marathas, was beaten by *Madhu Rao* in the west. The latter exacted a crore of rupees as compensation; *Haidar* refused it; *Marathas* pushed forward again. *Haidar spent night drinking, was entangled in the Western Ghats,* complete rout of same (cf. p. 116). Haidar fled to *Seringapatam*, asked *help from the English* under the *treaty (of 1769)*; but *Sir John Lindsay*, sent out by Parliament to control the affairs of Madras, insisted upon *treaty with the Marathas* and upon leaving Haidar Ali in the lurch. In consequence of *"this deliberate breach of faith," Haidar Ali* and his *son Tipu Sahib swore on the Koran everlasting hatred for the English* and to crush them. *Haidar* bought himself peace from the Marathas by *immediate payment of 36 lakhs of rupees*, and a *cession of territory* promising an annual income of 14 lakhs.

. . . .

V. WARREN HASTINGS' ADMINISTRATION, 1772-1785

April 13, 1772. *Warren Hastings* commenced his function as chosen Governor of Bengal; [Parliament] appointed the *members of the Council: General Clavering, Colonel Monson, Mr. Barwell, Mr. Francis*; [Hastings] transferred *central office* of the *Revenue Administration from Murshidabad to Calcutta*; made some alterations quoad *courts of justice* established by Clive (1765), but did not abolish what for the *ryots* was a *ruinous system of farming the revenues.*

1773. The *Reconstruction Act* passed; thereby Hastings became first *Governor-General.* At the same time, the *Supreme Court of Calcutta* was established by *13 George III c. 63*, and *late 1773* saw arrival of the *judges*, fellows *absolutely ignorant of Hindu customs* and regarding themselves as *chiefs of the entire government* [in India]. *In the same year, the infamous Rohilla war: Shuja-ud-daula, Nabob of Oudh*, informed *Warren Hastings* that the Rohillas did not pay him the *tribute of 40 lakhs* promised at the time of the Marathas' retreat to the Deccan (1773); the English should have this money [he said] if they helped him to reduce the Rohillas. On advice of the [Calcutta] Council, *Hastings* accepted it and made *treaty with the Nabob*, under which, if the war were successful, *he was to be allowed to buy, for 50 lakhs of rupees, the districts of Kora and Allahabad* which cost the Company a great deal without yielding any surplus. The brave chieftain of the Rohillas, *Hafiz Rahmat*, offered to pay the Nabob of Oudh all the outlays entailed by the Maratha war; but the latter demanded the *enormous sum of 200 lakhs*, which the Rohillas refused to pay, of course.

April 23, 1774. The united Oudh and British troops entered Rohilkhand, battle, in which the brave Rohillas almost exterminated and Hafiz Rahmat killed; the robbers left Rohilkhand after desolating it in addition.

1774-1775. *Disorders at Calcutta*; intrigues of a *majority of the Council* (above all *Francis*), the *judges* and the *Directorate* [of the Company] *at London* against Hastings.

1775. The Resident installed by Hastings with *Nabob of Oudh* was replaced with *Mr. Bristow* (appointed by the Directors). The fellow demanded—that was his first act—*payment of all the Nabob's arrears to the company within 14 days*. Hastings denounced this act of impolicy. Idem *Bristow* issued the *British troops* order to leave Rohilkhand at once; Hastings remonstrated; Bristow showed him *his secret instructions* from the London Directors; such orders could go only straight via *Governor-General*; *Hastings* wrote a solemn protest.

In the same year, *Shuja-ud-daula*, Nabob of Oudh, died; his son *Asaf-ud-daula* wrote to Calcutta, [asking] for support of the Company. *Francis*, through his majority in Council, forced Hastings to send *Asaf-ud-daula* order saying that all relations with Oudh were at end and *Asaf*'s succession must be based on *new treaty with the Company*, under which *Benares*, the most sacred city of India, should *absolutely* be ceded [to the Company] (see p. 120, note). Nabob had to give in while protesting.

The Begums of Oudh. Nabob's *zenana* (*serail*) was searched after his funeral, and rupees to the value of £2 million were found; the new Nabob took it as public money, but *Bristow* resolved that he should restore it to the *begums*, who claimed it as private inheritance. Thus Nabob unable to pay arrears to his troops; terrible mutiny; said to have cost the lives of 20,000 men!

In the *Calcutta Council*, *Francis* (with Clavering and Monson) did all to ridicule and exasperate Hastings, and *even appealed to the natives* to this end. At home he was abetted by the Directors, who kept ready a list of all his frivolous charges against Hastings. One major charge was a *fact unheard-of in India—execution of the Brahmin Nunkomar for forgery* (but this was handiwork of the *Supreme Court*, which in its blockheadedness applied *English law*, thereby turning into crime punishable by death what under Hindu law is a slight misdemeanour). *Francis* accused Hastings, saying he had wanted to get Nunkomar out of his way because the latter had *charged him with embezzlement*; later discovered that Nunkomar's charge a fabrication, the letter upon which the evidence depended being a forgery!

1776. In private letter to his London agent, *Hastings* mentioned his intention to resign; the agent let it out; but through *Colonel Monson's death* Hastings received *casting vote in Council*, wrote therefore to the London agent that he would stay; *Directors*, however, declared that *he had resigned.*

1777. Supported by this arbitrary act of the Directors, *General Clavering* sought as senior member of the Council to seize the insignia of power. Hastings treated him as usurper, shut the gates of Fort William against him, *Supreme Court* took action in Hastings' favour, Clavering *pegged out* with rage. In order not to hinder *Barwell's* intended resignation, *Francis* promised Hastings not to exploit the *majority in the Council* won in this manner; as soon as Barwell was gone, he did the opposite; Hastings accused him of deceit; duel between the two, in which Francis was wounded; the latter returned soon after to England, and Hastings had peace for a while; but *earlier*—

1772-1775—*Maratha affairs*; *1772*, *Madhu Rao*, the *Peshwa*, died. Succeeded by his brother *Narayan Rao*, at once murdered by *Raghoba.*

1773. *Raghoba* seized the throne; made war on the *Nizam*, who bought peace for 20 *lakhs of rupees*. Two statesmen, *Nana Pharnavis* and *Sakkaram Bapu*, set on throne an infant taken from the *zenana* and reputed posthumous child of Madhu Rao—under title of *Madhu Rao II*; the two fellows seized helm of state as regents.

1774. *Raghoba* utterly routed the two regents; but instead of marching to *Poona*, he went to *Burhanpur* and from there to *Gujarat* to ask co-operation of his countryman, the *Gaekwar*.

The *house of the Gaekwar* of *Gujarat*: *forefather—Pilaji Gaekwar* (under allegiance to the Peshwa)—*d. 1732*. Succeeded by *Damaji Gaekwar*, his son; extended his territory; made himself independent of Peshwa; *d. 1768*; three sons left after his death: *Govind Rao*, *Sayaji*, and *Fateh Singh*. *Govind Rao and Fateh Singh* disputed the throne; *Raghoba* sided with *Fateh Singh*, was supported in this by the great Maratha chieftains, *Holkar and Sindhia*.

1775. *Nana Pharnavis* through intrigues detached Holkar and Sindhia from that alliance; they withdrew. *Raghoba* now sent overtures to the English in *Bombay*; the *Government of Bombay* on its own hook made with Raghoba—

March 6, 1775—*Treaty of Surat*. By its terms: (1) the English to assist Raghoba to regain the Peshwa's throne; (2) Raghoba to cede *Salsette* (island) and *Bassein* (excellent port near Bombay) for trade purposes to the English, to pay annually *37 lakhs to the Bombay Government*. —The treaty *unconstitutional*: the *Regulating Act of 1773* provided that "the *subordinate presidencies*" (those of *Bombay* and *Fort St. George*, i.e., Madras), in the particular "cases of *concluding treaties* and *applying revenues, levying and employing forces*, and, in general, in all matters of civil and military administration, are placed under the superintendence of the *Governor-General of Bengal.*" Bombay Government could thus not make treaty without [the authorization of] Hastings and the Calcutta Council; Raghoba's subsidy, too, to be made payable, not to *Bombay Government* as was the case, but to Company as a whole. On these grounds, Francis forced Hastings to annul the treaty, thus involving the English in great troubles.

1775. *First Maratha War.* Colonel *Keating*, at head of British troops of Bombay, was ordered to effect junction with Raghoba; he was *attacked by the regents' army* on the *River Mhye*; had complete victory at *Arras* near Baroda; the Maratha army fled to the *Narbada*; *Fateh Singh*, marching out of Gujarat, effected junction with Keating. Success complete. —But, to spite Hastings, the *Treaty of Surat* [was] declared null and void by *majority* of the Council, and *circular* issued *to native princes* (!) *against Bombay Government*! The *Regency at Poona* then demanded restitution of *Salsette* and *Bassein*. *Colonel Upton*, acting on behalf of the Company, refused, [saying that] *Raghoba* was lawful *Peshwa*. *Upton*, on behalf of the Bombay Government, declared war on the Marathas. Thereupon the regents offered treaty, and idem *Upton*, who had just proclaimed Raghoba to be the lawful Peshwa, concluded with *Nana Pharnavis* and *Sakkaram Bapu* as representatives of the Maratha State—

March 1, 1776—*the treaty at Purandhar* (near Poona): *British army to quit the field* on condition of keeping *Salsette* and giving up all other territory formerly owned by the Marathas; British to receive 12 lakhs a year and to have the *revenues of* [the district of] *Bharoch* as long as they recognized *Madhu Rao II* as *Peshwa*. *Raghoba* was dropped, should receive 3 lakhs a year from the Marathas if he stayed *beyond the Godavari*. *Bombay Government*, however, insisted on *Surat Treaty*, broke treaty of Purandhar, offered Raghoba refuge in Surat, marched army to *Bharoch*. Regency proclaimed war; the British paraded Raghoba at Bombay. Shortly afterwards, *Bombay Government* received *message from the Court of Directors at home*, rejecting Treaty of Purandhar and recognizing that of Surat.

1778. *Maroba Pharnavis*—cousin of the Regent *Nana Pharnavis*—by agreement with *Sakkaram Bapu* (who, however, intrigued secretly in Raghoba's favour) formed a party at court with *Holkar*. This party appealed to *Bombay Government*; the latter granted its requests and wrote to Calcutta. *Hastings* approved because *Nana Pharnavis* was pro-French, and because the Company recognized Raghoba's title under *Treaty of Surat.* —*Nana Pharnavis* retired to Purandhar, bribed Holkar to leave the alliance, gathered army on behalf of *Madhu Rao*, defeated Maroba and Sakkaram, killed the first, and imprisoned the second at *Poona*, whither he marched after victory. *Bombay Government* [declared] war on him, after previous treaty with Raghoba.

1779. *Second Maratha Campaign. Colonel Egerton* was sent to attack *Poona*, but was hampered by *civilians* (whose chief was *General Carnac*). Before Poona, the *civil commissioners* grew funky and, contrary to Raghoba and Colonel Egerton, *ordered them to retreat*; the Regent's cavalry attacked them at once; brave Captain Hartley fought in rear-guard and the civilians "took to their heels" in front. At night, their army encamped at *Vargaon*, their camp was shelled, panic-stricken commissioners implored *Sindhia*, leading the enemy troops, to spare their lives! and to save them, hence to let them retire!

January 1779. *Convention of Vargaon*; the army of Bombay allowed to withdraw, extraditing *Raghoba* (anticipating this cowardice of the commissioners, he surrendered to Sindhia of his own free will) and *giving up every acquisition made during the last five years. Supreme Government* enraged by the news; proposed new treaty. Meanwhile *Raghoba* decamped to *Surat*, where *Colonel Goddard* the chief in command. *Nana Pharnavis* demanded Raghoba's extradition, Goddard refused, new war.

1779. *Third Campaign. Goddard* [went] *to Gujarat*, was joined there by Fateh Singh and Raghoba, [they] captured *Ahmadabad*; there they were opposed by the Marathas under *Holkar and Sindhia*, who were beaten and, during the rains, pitched cantonments on the Narbada.

1780. *Hastings* ordered a *small force to be formed under Major Popham* for demonstration against *Sindhia's possessions near Agra. Popham* took *Gwalior*, fortress on an almost perpendicular rock of great height. Then Popham's little corps was reinforced and, under command of General *Carnac*, made successful *night attack* on the Maratha camp; *Sindhia* fled, leaving all his stores behind him.

Late 1780. *Grand Confederacy between Marathas and Mysoreans to oust the English from India. Holkar, Sindhia, and Peshwa* (i.e., in fact, Nana Pharnavis) were to attack *Bombay, Haidar Ali to march on Madras*, and *Madhoji Bhonslay, Raja of Nagpur* (Berar), to attack Calcutta. The outcome was (see pp. 128, 129)—

May 17, 1782—*Treaty of Salbai* (*in Gwalior*): The English to restore all territory acquired since Treaty of Purandhar (*1776*), *Raghoba* to renounce all hostilities, receive 3 lakhs of rupees a year, and choose his own place of residence. *Haidar Ali* to *release all English prisoners within six months and relinquish all his conquests*; if not, *to be attacked by the Marathas.*

Haidar Ali. In *1770*, he had bought off the Marathas; stayed at rest. In *1772*, after murder of *Narayan Rao* by *Raghoba* and the subsequent disorders, he subjugated *Kurg* with unnecessary cruelty; *by 1774* he had reconquered all the districts wrested from him by the Marathas. In *1775*, he took *Bellary* from *Basalat Jang* (the Nizam's brother) and in *1776* destroyed *Savanur* (near Dharvas, Bombay Presidency), raj of *Morari Rao*, the Maratha chieftain. Futile attempt by *Poona Regency* to crush him.

1778. *Kingdom of Mysore was extended to the Kistna River.*

1779. *War declared between England and France*; Haidar declared for France. *English conquered Pondicherry and Mahé from the French.*

1780. *Haidar Ali* joined the *Grand Confederacy*, prepared *attack on Madras.*

1780. *Second Mysore War*. On *July 20*, *Haidar* marched through Chengama Pass into the *Carnatic*, devastated it, committed atrocities; smoke of the blazing villages seen from Madras.—*English army* only 8,000 men, in three divisions, separated at considerable distances. *Colonel Baillie*, in attempting at Guntur to effect junction with *Sir Hector Munro*, Commander-in-Chief, was attacked on the way by *Tipu Sahib* with large troop of Maratha cavalry; *Baillie* beat him back with difficulty and continued his march, but *Haidar*, interposed between him and Munro—

September 6, 1780—surrounding Baillie's force, *annihilated them almost to a man* near little village of Pollilore.— *Late* in *1780*, Haidar captured *Arcot*.

January 1781. *Sir Eyre Coote*, with reinforcements, arrived by sea from Calcutta; attacked Haidar at *Porto Novo*, near *Cuddalore*, with signal victory.

July 1781. *Bengal contingent under Colonel Pearse*, assisted by the *Raja of Nagpur* on its march through Orissa, arrived at *Pulicat*, effected junction with Coote, and together they gave *Haidar indecisive battle near little village of Pollilore* (*near Pulicat*).

September 27, decisive victory of Coote near *Solingur* (*in North Arcot, Madras Presidency*); later, during the rains, he went into cantonments near Madras.

Late 1781. *Lord Macartney*, *President* in Madras (*in lieu of Sir Thomas Rumbold*). His first act, *storming and razing of the Dutch fortress of Negapatam* and *destruction of the Dutch factories there*; this on *secret orders from Court of Directors, jealous of increasing Dutch trade in the South*. Also, slight success of the English at *Tellicherry*. *Haidar Ali* gave up *attempts on Carnatic* in order to attack the *Malabar coast*.

1782. *French fleet*, met, not far from *Porto Novo*, an *English fleet* returning after reduction of the *Dutch harbour of Trinkomali in Ceylon*; the naval action indecisive; *French* landed with small force at *Pondicherry*, and joined *Haidar Ali*.

July 1782. Two indecisive *naval engagements not far from Negapatam*.—A *French force* landed at *Point de Galle* (*Ceylon*), marched to *Trinkomali*, *retook the town, and destroyed the* [English] *garrison there*. *Admiral Hughes'* attempt against French fleet off Ceylon futile; *Hughes* [took fleet] *to Bombay*, leaving *the French masters of the seas*.

Towards end of 1782, *Tipu Sahib* attacked the *English entrenched camp* at *Palghat* (*near Coimbatore*); he failed in his first attempt at storming, and blockaded the camp till *December 7*, when he got word of *sudden death of Haidar Ali*, and marched with all his troops to Mysore.

December 6, 1782. *Death of Haidar Ali, 80 years old.* His Minister, the celebrated financier *Purnaiya*, kept his death secret till Tipu arrived.

. . . .

December 1782. *Accession of Tipu Sahib*; [he] found splendid army of 100,000 men, and immense treasure in money and jewels.

March 1, 1783. *Tipu*, who had first quietly consolidated his powers, went off to western coast to operate against *Mangalore*.

Early June 1783. *Bussy*, now in *command of all the French forces east of the Cape of Good Hope*, landed at *Cuddalore* with a French contingent, found *Tipu* gone to western coast and Haidar Ali dead; he was at once attacked by *General Stuart* (successor of Sir Eyre Coote);

June 7, 1783, an *outpost of Cuddalore* taken by English with heavy loss.—Same day, not far from Cuddalore, *naval engagement*, in which *Admiral Hughes* was worsted and put back to Madras to refit, while the French victor, *Suffrein*, landed 2,400 marines and sailors to form a brigade attached to Bussy's army.

June 18, dashing sortie of the French (with *Sergeant Bernadotte*, later King of Sweden, present) repulsed; then came *news of peace between England and France*, whereupon General Stuart returned to Madras; *Bussy* strengthened his position. Meanwhile *Bombay Government* had sent expedition, which captured *Bednore* and many other places on Malabar coast. *Tipu* marched down, *retook Bednore*, threw the garrison into prison, and then besieged *Mangalore* (1,800 men) with 100,000 men and 100 guns; it had to *capitulate after nine months' resistance*.—Simultaneously *Colonel Fullarton* led expedition from *Madras to Mysore*, took *Coimbatore*, and was marching on *Seringapatam* when he was recalled by *Lord Macartney*, who doltishly (see p. 133) began *peace negotiations*.—The first overtures based on mutual cessation of hostilities; Macartney *recalled the English* *troops, Tipu continued* to ravage the country round; [he] man-handled the commissioners and forbade them to retire until they signed *Treaty of Mangalore* at his dictation, on the basis of mutual restitution of conquests.

1770-1775. *Mr. Wynch, President of Madras. Sordid Tanjore business*[1] (p. 134).

1775-1777. *Lord Pigot, President of Madras.* This "aged" chap took the liberty (under order of the Directors) of not only reinstating the *Raja* of *Tanjore* in the raj stolen from him by *Mohammed Ali, "the Company's Nabob"* (of the Carnatic) in *1776*, but also intervening in the *corruption and peculation* in the various branches of public service; then there was, in particular, *his investigation* against a *certain Paul Benfield* because of a *fraudulent claim* of that "dog" to *a part of the revenues of Tanjore*. The *Council*, always opposed to the President, insulted him violently, he *suspended* two *members of the body*, the majority *shut up. Pigot* in gaol, *kept him in close confinement* till he died. This—the murder of the President!—went unpunished!

1777-1780. *Sir Thomas Rumbold, President of Madras.* The intrigues against him (pp. 135-138), he was succeeded by *Lord Macartney*, who arrived in *late 1781*.

1783-1785. *End of Warren Hastings' Administration. Hastings*, persecuted on all sides, made *violent displays of temper*. The *Supreme Court* obnoxious, considered itself supreme over all the departments of the Administration, posed as *"censor" of the acts of the Government*. The Government had passed regulations to treat the *zemindars* as mere *collectors of revenues, liable to arrest and punishment in case of default*; the *English judges* followed this rule with great impetuosity, often seized *powerful, so-called zemindari rajas*, threw them into prison, and *treated them like common felons* for some slight defalcation. Thus the zemindars' credit was impaired, *ryots often refused to pay them their rents*; hence still

[1] Under the Wynch Administration, Tanjore was captured and sacked — nominally by the Nabob of the Carnatic with help from Company troops, but in reality by the Company and British usurers. The greatest part of the booty fell into the hands of the Nabob's private "creditors," which was deeply resented by the Company's Court of Directors in London.

more *arbitrary persecutions and exactions by the zemindars towards the ryots*!

Under *charter of George I* (*1726*) and that of *George III* (*1773*), appointing *the Supreme Court*, all the *common law of England* was *now in force in India*; the English blockheads adhered rigorously to it, and so *the natives* (cf. p. 139) were *hanged* for what under their law was nothing!

The Cossijurah case arose from the English system of *demanding bail from accused persons pending their trial*; in this case, in a *revenue cause* brought in the *Supreme Court* against the Raja (i. e., Zemindar) Cossijurah (pp. 139, 140) (the *bailiffs* in this case penetrated into the sanctuary of the *zenana* and actually carried off *the family idol as security for his appearance*). As Hastings protected Cossijurah, and issued an order that *the natives were not to consider themselves amenable to the Supreme Court in civil matters* unless they *bound themselves of their own free will to abide by its jurisdiction*, the Supreme Court took the liberty of summoning the *Council and Governor-General* for "contempt of Court." Hastings did not care a straw.

New remodelling of the Revenue Administration and "*Warren Hastings' Code*" (p. 140). (Among other things, *he separated revenue from civil administration*, calling the former "*provisional*" and the latter, "*district*" *courts*, and placed above both, as *court of appeal*, the "*Sadr Divan-i-Adalat*,"[1] in which he appointed *Sir Elijah Impey* Chief Justice.

1784. *Case of Chait Singh*, whom Hastings had made *Raja of Benares* (140, 141).

Case of Faizullah Khan. A *treaty* was made with *Asaf-ud-daula*, Nabob of *Oudh*, under which he was to *subsidize British force in Oudh*; [the force was] reduced and some rights mutually fixed; the *3d article of the treaty* referred to *Faizullah Khan*, *nephew of Hafiz Rahmat* (the Rohilla); he was bound by treaty to muster contingent of 3,000 men when he became chieftain of the Rohillas in order to swell the ranks of the Company's army;

[1] Supreme Civil Court of Appeal.

Hastings had lately demanded 5,000, which *Faizullah Khan* declared he could not provide. In his *treaty with Oudh, Article 3*, Hastings claimed that *Rohilkhand*, being mere *jagir* of Faizullah's "feudal lord," the Nabob of Oudh, should be taken [by the latter]; he [Faizullah Khan] regained it later by paying 15 lakhs of rupees; thereupon Hastings returned to Calcutta.

1785. [Hastings went back] *to England*, having resigned his post at Calcutta. His mishaps in England; *Pitt his enemy*; hence the declamations of *Burke* (Pitt's man) (cf. pp. 142, 143). *Hastings d. 1818 (86 years old)*. (One great crime of Hastings', besides his *annexation policy* which Pitt disliked, was the fact that he had *raised the salaries of the Company's servants in India* to put an end to the extortions of these "rabble", who looked for fortunes, not in their pay, but in the *rupees extorted from the Hindus*.)

. . . .

[The Affairs of the East India Company in Britain]

March 1780. The exclusive privileges of the East India Co., subject to prolongation every three years, expired; they were prolonged by Act of Parliament *till 1783*; the *Company* had to pay *£400,000* to the public funds in part payment of arrears due to the nation for loans from Government.—*A secret* (parliamentary) *committee* was set up to inquire into the war with Haidar Ali; a *second*, to examine the *petitions* sent in by the native Bengalese against violent acts of the *Supreme Council of Calcutta*.

April 9, 1782. *Mr. Henry Dundas, member of the Board of the East India Directors* (the *dirty fellow* who later, in *1806*, was as *Earl of Melville* prosecuted in Parliament on a charge of corruption, first a man of North and Fox, then of Pitt), violently denounced the conduct of affairs in India; in *May 1782*, he moved for *recall of Warren Hastings*, which was passed by Parliament, but *Court of Proprietors* in a general meeting *refused to permit the Directors to send out the order for recall*.

1782. *Lord North*'s Ministry had fallen; succeeded by that of *Shelbourne*; overthrown by *coalition of Fox and North in April 1783.*

1783. (*Coalition ministry* of *North and Fox.*) *Fox*'s "*India Bill*" brought forward. The *Company handed in petition for another loan* (the *first granted by Parliament in 1772*); this *second profession of poverty* stirred up great noise in the country. *In his bill, Fox proposed the following*: The *Company's charter to be suspended for four years*; in the meantime the *government of India to be carried on by seven commissioners*, parliamentary nominees; *all matters of trade to be managed by nine assistant commissioners, nominated by the Court of Proprietors*; the *zemindars to be recognized as hereditary landowners*; in *all matters of war and treaties, the Government of India to be subordinate to a Board of Control in England.* (The latter [stipulation] was later embodied in *Pitt's bill.* Lord *Wellesley* did not give a damn for it during his *Indian administration.*) *Fox's bill* passed the Lower House; *George III* ordered *the Peers to throw out the bill*, whereupon—

January 1784—*George III* dismissed *Fox and Co.*; *Pitt became head* of the new ministry; he was *friendly to the Company* and in many ways benefited their trade.

August 13, 1784. *Pitt's "India Bill"*, a *body of six members of the Privy Council* appointed to act as a *Board of Commissioners* for the *control of revenue matters* and a *Committee of Secrecy of three Directors* to receive and issue the orders of this Board. The *Court of Proprietors* to *have no power of government*. All *war matters and treaties* to be *conducted and concluded under the orders of the Board of Commissioners. Annexation policy to be repudiated. Every officer under the Government of India to deliver a schedule of his property on his return to England*, with a notice of the manner in which it was acquired. The *bill passed by great majority in 1784*; henceforth *the President of the Board of Commissioners was the real despotic Governor of India.* Scamp *Dundas* (Melville) was first tô hold this office.

First case brought before the *scamp Dundas*: the *debts of the Nabob of Arcot* (alias *Mohammed Ali, of the Car-*

natic). This *Mohammed Ali*, a libertine and reveller and debauchee of the worst kind, *borrowed large sums from private individuals*, whom he repaid *by assigning to them the revenues of considerable tracts of land*. The *lenders* (alias *English swindler usurers*) found this "very advantageous"; *it established* the "vermin" *at once in the position of large landowners* and *enabled them to amass immense fortunes by oppressing the ryots*; hence *tyranny*—the most unscrupulous, too—towards the native peasants of these *upstart European* (*i. e.*, *English*) *zemindars*! Entire Carnatic ruined by them and the Nabob.

1785. Louse *Dundas* (and the Board of Commissioners headed by him) took the matter in hand and settled it to the best interest of the blood-sucking English scoundrels. *On the pretext of releasing* the country (Carnatic) from the money-lenders' clutches, they proposed *appropriating £480,000 to the payment of the Nabob's debts*, so that the private *usurers* who had ruined the Nabob should be *paid off before the East India Co.*, who had done him great services. It was pointed out to the miserable Dundas in the *House of Commons* that *the plan would bring immense sums to the Benfields* and others *who had formed a perfectly unscrupulous crew, and had fraudulently plundered the Carnatic of its lawful revenues*. The wretched *Pitt Ministry triumphantly passed the bill*—even then!—*through the House*, and *Paul Benfield alone thereby received £600,000 out of the revenues of the Carnatic*! (This was the handiwork of the very same Dundas-Melville who later ended in the filthy business of 1806![1]) *Dundas*, the corruption man, divided the *debts into three classes*, the largest being the *consolidated loan of 1777*. The plan submitted by *Warren Hastings would have paid this off for* $1^1/_2$ *million, while Dundas*'s *scheme occasioned a payment of* 5 *millions*! And 20 years later (in *1805*), when the last of the old debts had been paid off, it transpired, as was to be expected, that *Mohammed Ali* meanwhile had contracted *a new*

[1] In 1806, Dundas (Melville) was tried in the House of Lords on a charge of embezzling large government sums appropriated to the Navy when he was First Lord of the Admiralty (1804-1805).

debt amounting to 30 millions! Then came a new inquiry which *lasted 50 years*, and *cost £1 million* before the *affairs of the Nabob* were *finally settled*. That was how the British Government—for it was they and not the Company who had held sway [in India] since Pitt's bill—treated the poor Indian people!

[VI.] LORD CORNWALLIS' ADMINISTRATION, 1785-1793

1785-1786. After Warren Hastings' retirement, *Sir John Macpherson*, the senior member of the Council at Calcutta, became Governor-General pro tem.; through financial reform he reduced the government debt by £1 million. *Lord Macartney* was to have been nominated *Governor-General*, but was at once shelved because of *opposition to Dundas* in Parliament.

1786. *Cornwallis* arrived in Calcutta.—*Asaf-ud-daula*, Nabob of Oudh, begged for reduction of the expenses imposed on him *for maintenance of a British contingent in his territories*; Cornwallis reduced them *from 74 lakhs to 50* against the advice of the *Resident*, who said that Asaf would *spend* the surplus *on dancing girls and hunting expeditions*.—*Nana Pharnavis* made alliance with Nizam and prepared openly for war against *Tipu*, who appeased him by paying 45 lakhs.

1788. British troops annexed the *Guntur Circars*. The fact is that, under *Treaty of 1768*, Nizam had promised the Guntur Circars to the Company on death of the Governor of that province, *Basalat Jang*, who died in *1782*.—Nizam now demanded that the English should *fulfil the other part of the treaty* as well, that is, *conquer the Carnatic Balaghat from Haidar Ali's family*, so that he could pay *chauth* to the Marathas out of its revenues! But *none other than the English* had in *two successive treaties* recognized Haidar and Tipu as sovereigns of the *Carnatic Balaghat*! Cornwallis—

1788—promised the Nizam aid of British troops against any Power not in alliance with England, and *transfer of the Carnatic Balaghat as soon as it became English*! *Tipu Sultan's fury* at "*this double-dealing*" by Cornwallis!

The *Raja of Travancore*, ally of the East India Co., had bought *two towns from the Dutch at Cochin* and fortified them; the Chief of *Cochin*, vassal of Tipu, declared on the latter's order that the two towns belonged to him. The Raja appealed to the English, and the Chief of Cochin, to Tipu; the latter attacked the lines of Travancore, but was defeated by the Raja.—*Declaration of war between Tipu and the English.*

1790. *Cornwallis' "Tripartite Treaty,"* namely, offensive and defensive alliance with *Nana Pharnavis and the Nizam.*

1790-1792. *Third Mysore War* (in 1791, *Cornwallis* himself was in command). After the outwalls of Seringapatam had been stormed (*February 1792*), *Tipu* submitted; he had *to cede half his territory*, to pay the allies *£ 3 million for war expenses*, put two of his sons under British protection as *hostages*, and pay *30 lakhs of rupees to the Marathas.* The *Company* took for themselves *Dindigul* and *Baramahal* with country round and *some* land about Bombay; of the remainder of Tipu's territory, *Peshwa* received one-third (including the Carnatic Balaghat) and the Nizam, another third. *Charge in the House of Commons* against Cornwallis over his *annexation policy* fell through; moreover, he was created *Marquis.*

September 1793. *Pondicherry*, last and most important possession of the French, *taken by Colonel Brathwaite. . . .* Cornwallis returned to England.—His judicial reforms (pp. 156-158).

1784-1794. *Career of Sindhia.* He acquired great power in *southern India* through the *Treaty of Salbai* (in Gwalior) of 1782 (see p. 93).[1]

1784. Sindhia went to Delhi, made the puppet Emperor, *Shah Alam* (the once gallant Shah Zada, son of Alamgir II), give him the title of "*Executor-General* of the Empire" and chief command of the royal forces, and to present him with the *provinces of Agra and Delhi.*—[He] *attacked the Rajputs*, was terribly defeated; his "royal" forces deserted en masse to the enemy.

[1] P. 86 of this edition.

1787. *Sindhia* attacked by *Ismail Beg* (*nephew of Mohammed Beg*, the former Executor-General); Ismail took Agra, was reinforced with strong *band of Rohillas* under *Ghulam Kadir* (son of Zabita Khan). Sindhia marched from Delhi; attacked the allies, was defeated; the Rohillas marched north; *Sindhia* beat Ismail Beg's little army. But meanwhile the Rohillas—wild marauders—had taken and sacked *Delhi*, raged and plundered for two months, and finally blinded *Alam Shah*, taken prisoner by them; Ismail Beg now allied himself with Sindhia.

1788. These two allies jointly took Delhi; *Alam Shah* was restored to throne, *Ghulam Kadir* tortured to death, Ismail Beg put off with valuable jagir. Sindhia—virtual ruler in Delhi—formed splendid sepoy army under *French, English, and some Irish officers*, established large foundries, cast innumerable guns, etc., etc.

1791. Successful *campaign by Sindhia against the Rajputs.*— In order to transfer the *Mogul Empire* to *Marathas*—

1792—he made *Shah Alam* transfer the title of *Hereditary Deputies to himself and his heirs* and the title of *Wakil-ul-Mutlak* (*Regent of the Empire*), to the *Peshwa*; he himself went to *Poona*, invested with this dignity the *Peshwa*, who in his own state made him equal in dignity to his Vizier, *Nana Pharnavis.* From then on, intrigues between this "deepest politician of the age" and Sindhia and his descendants were the point round which the subsequent history of the Marathas turned.

1793. *Holkar*, second in power of the Maratha nobility, *defeated by Sindhia* in war; the latter now became *absolute master of Hindustan.*

1794. Mahdaji *Sindhia* died suddenly; succeeded in all his titles and offices by *his grand-nephew, Daulat Rao Sindhia.*

. . . .

1786-1793. *Parliamentary Proceedings: 1786, bill passed,* empowering the *Governor-General to legislate personally without consulting his Council*; *Wellesley*, who later became Governor-General, found that "comme il faut"; *act passed* in order to spare [the Governor-General] the hamperings which had harassed *Warren Hastings*.

1788. *Declaratory Act*, prompted by collision between the *Board of Directors* of the Company and the *Board of Commissioners* representing the Crown; Ministry ordered enrolment of four new regiments for special service in India, *Company* refused to pay for their embarkation and maintenance. *Board of Commissioners* ordered the Company to provide the fund, *Directors* declared they held chief governing power in matters of finance. *As early as 1784, Pitt* had stated (and now did so again) that the intention of the Cabinet was at some future date *to transfer the whole of the governing power in India to the hands of the nation*. Turbulent debates in the House. The *Declaratory Act* enforced only the *Act of 1784*, and gave the Board of Commissioners *power to direct the conduct of the Company* in all matters of state. In *1793, privileges of the Company were extended for* 20 *years* by a new charter.

. . . .

[Confiscation of Ryot Lands in Favour of the Zemindars, 1793][1]

Bengal's land was recognized as private property of the zemindars during the first—

1793—*cadastral* survey ordered by the Governor-General of Bengal, Lord *Cornwallis* (his administration, *1786-1793*). (In *1765*, the English found the zemindars—"collectors of public revenue"—claiming the position of *zemindari rajas*, which power they had gradually assumed during the decay of the Mogul Empire.) (The *hereditary* nature of their tenures was due to the fact that the Great Moguls did not care for the mode of

[1] The passage which appears under this subheading—from here to the dotted line on p. 101—is from the same note-book of Marx's (pp. 68 and 70), the section entitled "(E) British Domination and Its Influence on Indian Public Property."

tenure, so long as the *annual tax* was handed in; the latter was *a certain fixed sum*, considered as the annual produce of the district above its own exigencies. All that the zemindar made over and above this belonged to himself, *therefore he fleeced the ryots.*) Their [the zemindars'] claim to be considered *rajas* was due to the wealth of land and money they had amassed by looting, their maintenance of troops, and assumption of state. The English Government ([from], 1765) treated them as mere *subordinate tax-collectors*, placed them under legal responsibility, and made them *liable to be thrown into prison or deposed from office* on the slightest failure of regular payment. *On the other hand, the condition of the ryots was not raised*; indeed, they were humbled and oppressed still more, and *the whole revenue system was thrown out of order.*

1786. The Directors, *as a matter of policy*, ordered a new engagement to be entered into with the *zemindars* under distinct understanding that whatever benefits they were granted, they had them, not by *right*, but only through *favour* of the *Governor* in *Council*; *Commission* appointed to inquire into, and report on, the *condition of the zemindars*; *ryots* refused to testify, fearing the vengeance of the zemindars; the latter evaded all inquiries, and the work of the commissioners was at a deadlock.

1793. *Lord Cornwallis* gave up the Commission and suddenly, without warning, *passed* a motion in the Council, which at once assumed the force of law, that the zemindars were to be henceforth considered *as possessing all* [the territory] *they claimed . . . as hereditary owners of all the soil* of the district, *paying annually, not their quota of public taxes which they collected for the Government*, but a *sort* of tribute into the Treasury! *Mr. Shore*, subsequently *Sir John Shore*, the scamp Cornwallis' *successor in office*, spoke strenuously in Council *against the wholesale destruction* of Indian tradition; and when he saw that the majority of the Council was determined (just to *get rid* of the burden of constant legislation and of perpetual disputes concerning the status of the Hindus) to proclaim the zemindars owners of the land, he proposed *decennial settlements*, but Council declared for *permanency*. The *Board of Commissioners* applauded their resolution and—

1793—*under the Premiership of Pitt* passed the Bill for the "*permanent establishment of the zemindars of India as hereditary landowners.*" This decision was promulgated at *Calcutta in March 1793* to the utter delight of the amazed zemindars! The measure was as *illegal* as it was sudden and unexpected, for the English were supposed to be legislating for the Hindus as a race and, *as far as possible, administering to them their own laws.* Simultaneously the English Government passed several laws *giving the ryots remedies in the civil court against the zemindars, and protecting them from increase of rent.* Those were *nugatory, dead-letter* [laws], considering the state of the country; for the *ryots were so absolutely* at the mercy of their landlords that they seldom dared to raise a finger in self-defence.—One of the measures mentioned above was *a regulation fixing the rents of the lands for ever.* It enacted that a written *pottah*, being a document containing the conditions of tenure and *the amount of the sum to be paid annually as rent*, should be given to the ryot. This regulation allowed the zemindar *to increase the value of the estate by the cultivation of fresh lands* and *to increase the rental on fields cultivated with the higher-priced kinds of grain.*

1793. Thus *Cornwallis and Pitt artificially expropriated the rural population* of Bengal (p. 161).

1784. The British legislature decisively interfered to regulate "the affairs of the East India Co." and of the British "*possessions in India.*" To this end, *Act of the 24th George III. c. 25* was passed, which became the groundwork of the Constitution of British India. The Act established the *Board of Commissioners for the Affairs of India*, commonly called the *Board of Control*, to superintend and control the *East India Co.* in the exercise of the political part of their *functions. Under Section 29* of the Act, *the Company* were required to investigate the *truth of certain complaints*, which had prevailed, of oppressions inflicted on *divers rajas, zemindars, poligars, and other landholders in British India*, and to establish, "*upon principles of moderation and justice, according to the laws and Constitution of India*," permanent rules for the future collection of the territorial revenue.

1786. *Marquis Cornwallis* [came] to India as Governor-General; this fellow at once effected, conformably to the instruction of the *Court of Directors and Board of Control* (brought by him from England)—

1787—*reunion of the functions of civil justice and criminal police with those of financial management in the person of the collector*, by making him both the magistrate and the judge *of the provincial civil court* (*Mufassal Divan-i-Adalat*), but the *proper court of the collector* as judge of revenue cases—remained separated from the *Divani*[1] *Court, over which he presided*; appeal from the latter court went to the *Sadr Divan-i-Adalat*, and from his [the collector's] revenue court, only to the *Board of Revenue* sitting at Calcutta.

1793. According to Cornwallis' *permanent settlement* for the three provinces of *Bengal, Bihar, and Orissa*, where the amount of territorial revenues to be yielded by the three provinces was settled in perpetuity *on an average of the past collections, a default of payment was to be supplied by a proportionate sale of land*, while the zemindar "*could recover his own dues from the renter only by means of a legal process.*" The land-holders complained that they were *thus thrown on the mercy of the inferior renters*, since the Government annually demanded from them, on pain of a privation of their land, what they could recover from their renters only by a tardy process of law. *New rules* were therefore established under which, in *certain* specified cases and with forms very carefully prescribed, a *power was granted* to the zemindar *of enforcing payment on his tenants by arrest*, while the *collector*, in similar

[1] Civil.

way, was invested with the same authority over the zemindar. This [was done] in *1812*.[1]

Results of the "settlement": First product of this plunder of *"communal and private property"* of the ryots: *whole series of local risings of the ryots* against the "landlords" [conferred on them], involving: in some cases, *expulsion of the zemindars and stepping of the East India Co. into their place* as owner; in other cases, *impoverishment of the zemindars* and *compulsory or voluntary sale of their estates to pay tax arrears* and *private debts*. Hence *greater part of the province's land holdings fell rapidly into the hands of a few city capitalists* who had spare capital and readily invested it in land.[2]

. . . .

VII. SIR JOHN SHORE'S ADMINISTRATION, 1793-1798

(He succeeded *per interim* at Cornwallis' retirement as senior member of the Council, and the *Board of Commissioners* confirmed him as *Governor-General for five years*.)

1793. At the instance of the Governor-General, the signers of the *Tripartite Treaty* of 1790 (against Tipu Sahib) were to sign a *Guarantee Treaty* as well, with the codicil that if *one of the three Powers went to war against Tipu Sultan* for an illegal object, the others should not be bound by the treaty. *Nana Pharnavis* refused to sign, *Nizam* accepted.

1794. *The Peshwa, and the Marathas generally, made war of plunder against the Nizam*; on the strength of *Tripartite Treaty*, he turned to *Sir John Shore* [for help], which the latter, afraid of the immense Maratha army, *refused*. The *Nizam* then *enlisted the good offices of the French*, who sent him *two battalions in aid*; besides,

---

[1] Cf. Harrington, *Elementary Analysis of the Bengal Laws and Regulations*; Colebrooke, *Supplement to the Digest of Bengal Laws and Regulations*.—*Author's note*.

[2] This paragraph has been taken from Marx's abstract of Kovalevsky's book. The abstract immediately follows Marx's chronological notes.

[he] raised body of *18,000 sepoys*, officered by *French adventurers*.

November 1794. Under *Peshwa*, the young *Madhu Rao II*, the Marathas, with *150 guns and 130,000 men*, marched into Central India. (*Daulat Rao Sidhia* contributed to that army 25,000 men under *General De Boigne*; the *Raja of Berar*, 15,000; *Holkar*, 10,000; the *Pindaris*, 10,000; *Govind Rao*, the Gaekwar, *5,000*; the *Peshwa*, 65,000.) Armies met at *Harda*.

November 1794. *Nizam Ali* sustained *great defeat*, gave way, committed himself *to pay at once £3 million*; to deliver over *lands to the value of £35,000* per annum, and to surrender *his ablest minister* as hostage in the Marathas' hands.—Rightly enraged by the "wanton neutrality" of the English, Nizam disbanded all *British troops* in his pay, recruited [a few] more *French battalions*, made *Raymond* their chief, assigned the French, by way of payment for a French contingent to be kept at Hyderabad, the lucrative *province of Kurpa*. Shore interfered because of the *piece of land on the borders of the Company's territory*. After some incidents the matter was left at that.

October 1795. *Suicide of Madhu Rao II*; he was succeeded by *his cousin*, clever and unscrupulous *Baji Rao* (*son of Raghoba*).—Intrigues between *Baji Rao*, *Nana Pharnavis, and Sindhia* (*Daulat Rao*) (cf. pp. 164-168) ended—

December 4, 1796—in *Baji Rao*, for some time displaced by his brother *Chimnaji*, being reinstated at *Poona* with *help from the Nizam*, *Pharnavis*, etc.; he now dismissed *Nana Pharnavis* and threw him into *deepest dungeon* of his palace; now he had to get rid of *Sindhia*; he publicly refused him the promised *jagir*, stirred up, through *Sarji Rao Ghatke* (treacherous officer of Sindhia), a *gruesome rebellion of Sindhia's troops at Poona* (of which Sindhia *knew nothing*), thus set the people of Poona against Sindhia, and sent him back north.

1796. *Mutiny of the Company's* (*not* the royal British) *officers in Calcutta*; they were *paid less* than the Company's civil service; they demanded *increase of pay*, etc. (see p. 168). This was eliminated through

Sir Robert Abercromby's (commander at *Cawnpore*) *intervention.* (It was second émeute[1] since the one *under Clive in 1766.*)

1797. The *Mayor's Court at Madras* (established by *George I in 1726*) abolished by Act *36 George III*; replaced by *Recorder's Court* on model of the *city of London Quarter Sessions.* (Mayor *nominal*, recorder *real* judge.) (See p. 169, n. 1.)

1797. Death of *Asaf-ud-daula, Nabob of Oudh* (after a life of indolence and debauchery). A *reputed son* of his, *Wazir Ali* by name, placed on throne by the *English.* He was later deposed and replaced by the English themselves with Asaf's brother *Saadat Ali*; the English made *treaty* with the latter: *10,000 British troops to garrison Oudh*; to be *maintained* [by the Nabob] by *annual payment* of *76 lakhs of rupees*, with the *fortress of Allahabad* for their headquarters; the *Nabob to make no treaties without the permission of the Governor-General.*

March 1798. *Sir John Shore* returned to England, and was made *Lord Teignmouth.*

. . . .

[VIII.] LORD WELLESLEY'S ADMINISTRATION, 1798-1805

On his arrival in Calcutta, *Tipu Sahib* was breathing revenge; *Nizam* had at *Hyderabad army of 14,000 French under Raymond* and 36 guns; *Sindhia* ruled at Delhi, with army of *40,000 sepoys*, officered by Frenchmen under *De Boigne*, with 460 guns. Treasury empty.

1799. *Fourth and Last Mysore War.* (Tipu Sahib had demanded and obtained *French* contingent from *Mauritius*, whereupon Wellesley declared war.) Wellesley secured from Nizam replacement of the *French troops* at Hyderabad by *British.* Peshwa, as well as Nizam, fulfilled their treaty obligations; *Sindhia* and *Raja of*

[1] Mutiny.

Nagpur refused Wellesley aid and alliance; English *Board of Commissioners* consented to war against Tipu.

February 5, 1799. Wellesley commenced his march on Mysore with 20,000 English, 100 guns, 20,000 sepoys and native cavalry; *Harris*, Commander-in-Chief.—In the *battle at Malavelli* (in Mysore), where Tipu was defeated, *Colonel Wellesley* (who later became *Duke of Wellington*) appeared for the first time on Indian soil.

May 3,[1] 1799. *Seringapatam taken. Tipu Sahib's corpse* (shot through the head, etc.) found *near the breach.* (*Wellesley* was created marquis). Wellesley gave up *Mysore* to *child of five years*, sprung from the old *Hindu Dynasty of Mysore* (which Tipu had ousted), with *Purnaiya* for his minister. (That infant lived till *1868*, and was succeeded by his *adopted son*, four years old.) *Treaty made* with *Purnaiya* practically placed *Mysore* under English supremacy; *Mysore* had to keep a *military force* under *English discipline and orders*; raj to be considered as gift of the English Government; in case of maladministration, or non-payment of the *annual subsidy* for the military force, the Company was entitled to occupy *as much territory* as it deemed necessary for payment of the subsidy; [Mysore] to pay the *Company* an annual £310,000, out of which the Company gave annuity of £96,000 to Tipu's heirs, and out of the £240,000 annuity [paid by Mysore] to *Nizam* £28,000 was to be paid to the Chief Commander of the Mysore army (for that fellow had surrendered unconditionally) and £92,000, to *Peshwa*, who declined it. Hence the *land* was portioned between the *Nizam* and the *Company*.—Afterwards there [was] only one *serious rebellion* in *Mysore*, that of *Dhundia Wagh*; it was suppressed a few months later and he himself killed.—*Nizam* demanded *more British troops* to be sent to Hyderabad, and ceded for their maintenance what is still known as "*ceded districts.*"

[1] May 4, according to Wilks, *Historical Sketches of the South of India in an Attempt to Trace the History of Mysoor*, Vol. III, London, 1817.

1799. *Annexation of Tanjore* (see p. 175), founded 120 years earlier by Venkoji, brother of Shivaji.
Annexation of the Carnatic (pp. 176, 177).—In *1795*, spendthrift *Mohammed Ali*, "the Company's Nabob," died; *1799* saw death of his successor and son, the spendthrift *Umdat-ul-Umara*; his nephew, *Azim-ul-Umara*, was made Nabob by Wellesley, consented to *annexation of Carnatic* on promise *of annuity of one-fifth of the revenues* for his maintenance.

1799-1801. *Shameless annexation of part of Oudh.*

1800. *Wellesley* ordered the Nabob of Oudh, *Saadat Ali*, to disband his troops, replace them by *English troops* or *sepoys*, commanded by English officers, and to *shell out* for these *British regiments*! Meaning was: *to transfer the whole military command in Oudh to the Company*, and *to pay for its own enslavement* into the bargain! Saadat wrote in a *despatch* to Wellesley that he would resign in favour of one of his sons rather than sacrifice the *independence of the country* in that way! In despatch written in answer, Wellesley *told a lie*, [saying] that *Saadat Ali had realiter*[1] *abdicated*, that the whole *royal treasure* must now be *surrendered* and the *whole country proclaimed English*, and that each *subsequent Nabob* would *possess throne* only as *gift from the English Governor-General*. Thereupon Saadat Ali withdrew the abdication mentioned in his despatch only as an *intention*. Wellesley sent troops, *Nabob was compelled to give in*; he disbanded *large part of his own troops* and replaced them by British.

November 1800. Wellesley demanded disbandment of the rest of the native troops and, in view of their replacement by new British regiments, *increase* of the subsidy from 55 to 76 lakhs of rupees. Nabob protested in vain his "inability" to pay so high a tribute! Thereupon he freed himself from the tribute by *ceding* [to the British] *Allahabad*, *Azamgarh*, *Gorakhpur*, and *Southern Doab*, with some others, all together being of the annual value of £1,352,347. Commission superintended by *Henry*

[1] In fact.

Wellesley, the Governor-General's brother (*afterwards Lord Cowley*), settled the country.

1800. *Ruler of Kabul* was *Zaman* (son of *Timur Shah*, son of *Ahmad Khan Abdali*, who in *1757* took Delhi and in *1761*, after the Battle of Panipat, [re-] conquered *Kabul*[1] and [re-] established a Durani Dynasty there); he had been negotiating with *Tipu Sultan*, and the Company feared attack on his part; this was main reason why *Wellesley* annexed *Oudh* as check against hostile advance. Several times *Zaman* brought armies to the frontier, appealed as "*champion of Islam*" to Mohammedans in India, and even received promises from various Hindu rajas. Napoleon was plotting in the East as well; Calcutta's "office-boys" trembled at the combination: *France*, *Persia*, and *Afghanistan*. Hence the *embassy to Persia* under Captain *Malcolm*! [It] cost a mint of money; he "bought" everything from "*the Shah to the camel-driver*"; brought about the following *treaty*, signed at *Teheran*: King of Persia to *eject every Frenchman from Persia*; to discountenance all *attacks on India*, and oppose them by arms, if necessary; to *give all his patronage of foreign commerce to the English*.

1802. Wellesley tendered his resignation to Board of Commissioners, but at their insistance *stayed* [in India] till 1805. The fact is that he had quarrelled with Company because he wanted to extend the private traders' rights to India.

Beginning of the Century. Besides the English, [there was] *only one great power* [in India], that of the *Marathas*; these were divided into five principal parties, mostly at loggerheads with each other. (1) *Peshwa, nominal supreme chief of the Marathas*, was *Baji Rao*, reigning at *Poona*; the *smaller states, not listed here*, were half independent, half owing feudal submission to the Peshwa as their hereditary sovereign; (2) *Daulat Rao Sindhia*, [representing] strongest of the Maratha

[1] Here the book used by Marx contains an error, for the city in question was Kandahar and not Kabul. A number of British authors, such as James Mill, for some reason consider Kabul to have been the capital of Ahmad Shah, whereas he ruled and died in Kandahar.

families, was at *Gwalior* and in possession of *Delhi*, etc.; (3) *Jaswant Rao Holkar*, at *Indore*, mortal enemy of Sindhia; (4) *Raghoji Bhonslay*, Raja of Nagpur, willing to fight anybody for a consideration; (5) *Fatch Singh, Gaekwar of Gujarat*, who seldom joined in Maratha politics.

1800. *Nana Pharnavis* died in prison.—Sindhia left Poona because of Holkar's plundering of *city of Sagar* (in *Indore*, belonging to Sindhia) and, in company with *Amir Khan*, Rohilla chieftain, devastated *Malwa*, also belonging to Sindhia.—Sindhia's and Holkar's forces met at *Ujjain* (in Malwa), *Sindhia* was *defeated*; sent for aid to Poona and—

1801—received from there *forces* under *Sarji Rao Ghatke*; the allied forces on *October 14 defeated Holkar*, marched on his capital, Indore, sacked it, *Holkar* fled to *Khandesh*, devastated the surrounding country; advanced to *Chandor*, and thence announced to the Peshwa that he was coming with all his forces, claiming his protection against Sindhia.

1802. *Baji Rao*, who had atrociously murdered the young robber chieftain *Vittaji*, Holkar's brother, whom he had captured shortly before, saw this message merely as a screen to an open declaration of war. *Offer of the Company's arms* against Holkar by *Colonel Close*, the British Resident at Poona, was obstinately refused by the Peshwa; *Sindhia* moved up quickly, and *encamped near Poona.*

October 25, 1802, *great battle. Holkar won*; the Peshwa fled to Singar, about 50 miles from Ahmadnagar, thence to *Bassein* (belonging to the Company). During his two months' sojourn at Poona, Holkar set *Amrit Rao*, the Peshwa's brother, on the throne, while *Sindhia* [went] *north.*

1802. *Treaty of Bassein between Baji Rao and Colonel Close:* Peshwa *to maintain 6,000 British infantry with guns*; for their support to assign to the Company *certain districts in the Deccan*, yielding annual revenue of 25 lakhs[1] of rupees; to keep *no non-British Europeans*

[1] 26 lakhs, according to Smith, *The Oxford History of India*, 1923.

in his service; to refer all his claims against the Nizam and the Gaekwar to Governor-General as arbitrator; to make no political changes without his concurrence; both parties to consider themselves as mutually bound in a *defensive alliance*.—Indignation of all the Marathas at this "*subsidiary treaty*," which would *unmake their independence, acknowledging the English as a superior power*.—Hence *Sindhia's* measures; he [formed]—

1803—*Maratha confederation against the English*; it consisted of *Sindhia, Amrit Rao, Bhonslay* (Raja of Nagpur); *Holkar* consented to join, but *later failed to keep his promise*; the *Gaekwar* remained *neutral*.

GREAT MARATHA WAR, 1803-1805

April 17, 1803. Sindhia and Bhonslay met at Nagpur, marched at once to Poona to join Amrit Rao.—Lord Wellesley ordered up troops, and *General Wellesley* (Wellington), for the first time in actual command of armies, advanced *with the Mysore army* (about 12,000 men), by forced marches, to *Poona*, allegedly in order to restore *Baji Rao* to throne. *Holkar* returned to *Chandor*, *Wellesley* took *Poona*, *Amrit Rao* fled to *Sindhia's* camp.—The allied Marathas marched on Poona; *conferences* yielded nothing, but some months passed in the meantime. After giving all the necessary orders, General Wellesley recalled *Colonel Collins* from the allies' camp, and the *war began*.

On General Wellesley's orders, *General Lake* to attack at *Gwalior* Sindhia's reserve force commanded by *Perron*, while *two corps d'armée* were to take possession of *Sindhia's dominions in Bharoch* and of *Holkar's* in *Cuttack* (*Bengal Presidency*). About 3,000 men were left for the *defence of Hyderabad* and the *ceded districts*; *main army* with Wellesley, 17,000 men.

August 1803. Wellesley took *Ahmadnagar*, Colonel Woodington ditto *Bharoch*; *General Lake* launched attack on the fortress of *Aligarh* (Delhi Province) and on *September* 2 captured *fort*; *on September 4, the place capitulated.*

September 3,[1] **1803.** *Great battle of Assaye*; *the Marathas* beaten by General Wellesley.
Almost simultaneously, *Harcourt* took *Cuttack* (in the Bay of Bengal), and *Stephenson*, the *fort of Burhanpur* and *Asirgarh in the Satpura Hills. Sindhia* made a truce with Wellesley, who, joining Stephenson's force from Bharoch, marched against *Bhonslay's* strong *fortress of Gawilgarh.*

November 28,[2] **1803.** *Battle at Argaon* (*near Ellichpur*). *Wellesley won*, Bhonslay fled, *Colonel Stephenson* was sent on march against *Nagpur* (capital of Berar); *Bhonslay* begged for terms, hence—

December 18,[3] **1803**—*Treaty of Deogaon between Bhonslay and Mountstuart Elphinstone on behalf of the East India Co.*: English spared the territories of Berar; the Raja ceded *Cuttack* to the Company; gave several districts to the *Nizam*; excluded *all Frenchmen* and Europeans at war with England; [committed himself] to refer all differences to the Governor-General for arbitration.

September 14, *Lake*, who after taking Aligarh marched straight on Delhi, met, six miles from the city, *Sindhia's troops under French officers*, defeated the French, that *same evening took Delhi*, and replaced the blinded *Shah Alam* (83 years old) on the throne under *British protection.*

October 17, *Agra*, held by the *Raja of Bharatpur, capitulated* vis-à-vis Lake.—Lake marched out against large body of the enemy from the *Deccan and Delhi*; after terrible battle, Lake was victorious—at *Laswari* (*village 128 miles south of Delhi*); Sindhia *down.*

December 4,[4] **1803.** *Treaty of Anjangaon between Lake* (*acting on behalf of Company*) *and Sindhia*; Sindhia *ceded all his territories north of Jaipur* and *Jodhpur*; ditto *Bharoch* and *Ahmadnagar*; gave up *all claims on the Nizam, the Peshwa, the Gaekwar, and the Company*; had to acknowledge the independence of those

[1] September 23, according to Burgess.
[2] November 29, according to Burgess.
[3] December 17, according to Burgess.
[4] December 30, according to Burgess.

states recognized by the Company as independent; undertook to *dismiss all foreigners*, and to *submit* in *all disputes to the arbitration of the Company*.—The *Governor-General*, *Wellesley*, gave *Berar* to the Nizam, *Ahmadnagar* to the Peshwa, and reserved *Cuttack* for the Company; simultaneously he made *treaties* with the *rajas of Bharatpur*, *Jaipur*, and *Jodhpur* with the *Raja of Gohad* (in Sindhia's territory of Gwalior), to whom he [promised to give] the *city of Gwalior*, and with *Ambaji Inglia*, Sindhia's general.

Early 1804. *Holkar* (instead of joining the Maratha confederation in keeping with his promise, he had with 60,000 cavalry *plundered Sindhia's possessions*), began to invade the territory of the *Raja of Jaipur*, ally of the Britishers; hence the victorious armies of Wellesley and Lake drew near; *Holkar* retreated from Jaipur beyond the River *Chambal*, where he gave *Colonel Monson*, sent with small force in his pursuit, so sound a thrashing that Monson, having lost guns, baggage, camp equipage, and stores of the division, and *lost almost five battalions of infantry*, finally arrived at Agra with the miserable survivors.—*Holkar* now attacked—ineffectually—*Delhi*, and ravaged the country round; *General Lake* followed him in all haste and came up with his army.

November 13, 1804, *battle of Dig* (in territory of Bharatpur); *Holkar beaten*, fled to *Muttra* (*on the River Jumna, north of Agra*); *Fort Dig*, which belonged to the *Raja of Bharatpur* and had fired on the English during the battle, *taken by storm* after the victory.

1805. *Lake* attacked *Bharatpur without success*; nevertheless, the Raja came to terms with the English.—*Holkar joined Sindhia* who was now at the *head of a new combination of his own forces with those of Holkar, the Raja of Bharatpur*, and *Amir Khan the Rohilla*. The fact is that, when the *Governor-General*, Wellesley, had given the Raja of Gohad his old family seat of *Gwalior*[1],

[1] Here the book used by Marx contains an error. Wellesley promised to give Gwalior to the Raja of Gohad, but he did not intend to do so, and kept a British force there.

Sindhia protested that his General, *Ambaji Inglia*, had *concluded treaty with the English* and transferred the city to them *without reference to Sindhia. General Wellesley declared Sindhia was in the right*, but *Governor-General Wellesley* refused Sindhia demand to give him back Gwalior, and administered him a severe rebuke. This *led to a new confederation under Sindhia*, who again took the field with 40,000 men against the English, but Wellesley's successor, *Sir George Barlow, gave back Gwalior to Sindhia* and made new treaty with him.

July 20, 1805. *Governor-General Wellesley*, his tenure of office having elapsed, *sailed to England*.

Administrative reforms of Wellesley. In place of the *Sadr Divan-i-Adalat*, a court established by Lord Cornwallis in *1793* (*in lieu of the Supreme Court*), over which Governor-General and the members of the Council presided with *closed doors*, Wellesley—

1801—established a separate court *open to the public* and presided over by regularly appointed *chief justices*; the first of them was *Colebroke. In the same year, a Supreme Court* [was established] at *Madras* in place of the *Sadr Divan-i-Adalat*, on the principle extant in Calcutta previous to Cornwallis. This *court* lasted till *1862*, when it was superseded by the *High Court*. The *Recorder's Court*, introduced by *George III*, was abolished, and its powers were assumed by the *new chief justices and puisne judges* (by *Act 39 and 40 George* III c. 79. The same Act gave the new court power to deal with *insolvent debtors*, a sort of delinquents that till then had received no particular attention in India). The same Act extended *vice-admiralty jurisdiction to the chief courts at the presidency towns in India. Thus new European* (*English*) *element increased everywhere*.

Lord Wellesley established *great college at Calcutta*, named *College of Fort William*; it was to serve (1) as educational institution for *ignorant young civilians* sent out from England; (2) as *hall for discussions amongst the natives* upon matters of law and religion. The *Directors of the East India Co.* confined the agency of the college to the educational department. Simultaneously Company established the *College of Haileybury*, in England, for instruction of *writers* previous to their departure for India.

[IX.] LORD CORNWALLIS' SECOND ADMINISTRATION, 1805
(He arrived at Calcutta on July 20)

August 1, Cornwallis assumed the insignia of office; *his principle*, he declared, was that *of non-annexation*; said he would *give up all lands west of the Jumna*; *Lake* (who was created *Baron* and then, in *1807*, Viscount) remonstrated.

October 5, *old Cornwallis died*; he was succeeded by the senior member of the *Council*, *Sir George Barlow*, *rigid anti-annexationist*.

. . . . ,

[X.] SIR GEORGE BARLOW'S ADMINISTRATION, 1805-1806

Late 1805. *Treaty with Sindhia*: Sindhia received *Gohad* and *Gwalior* on condition of keeping the *Treaty of Anjangaon*; *Barlow guaranteed that the British Government would make no treaty* with any of Sindhia's tributary states in the Rajput territory without Sindhia's consent. After Sindhia's submission, *Holkar* left his camp and began, with his usual ruthless cruelty, to ravage the *country near the Sutlej*; *Lake* pursued him with aid of *Ranjit Singh*, the great trans-Sutlej chieftain; *Holkar* was utterly defeated, and fled, suing for a treaty.

January 1806. Lord Lake signed *treaty with Holkar*, under which this fellow had to renounce all claims to *Rampra*, *Tonk*, *Bundi*, and *all places north of the Bundi Hills*. Sir *George Barlow* refused to ratify the treaty which conferred *Bundi*—annexation!—to the *Company*; ordered the English troops to *withdraw from beyond the Chambal River*, whereupon *Holkar* at once ravaged the dominions of the *Raja of Bundi* again.—In the same way, *Barlow* left the *Raja of Jaipur*, English ally, a prey of the Maratha soldiery.—*Thereupon Lord Lake resigned all civil powers* in the hands of Barlow, declaring that he would never again sign *treaty* if immediately negatived afterwards at headquarters.

Holkar had mental alienation as a result of having murdered, in a fit of passion, his brother and his nephew; *died at Indore in 1811 in a state of insanity.*

1807. *Barlow* superseded by *Lord Minto*, who came to India, also *pledged to non-intervention*; Minto arrived at Calcutta on *July 31, 1807*; Barlow was transferred to the *Government of Madras.*

. . . .

[XI.] LORD MINTO'S ADMINISTRATION, 1807-1813

July 1807. *Mutiny at Vellore* (*Madras Presidency*), in fort of which *Tipu's sons* [were held] captive; mutiny in their behalf by their *Mysorean suite*; they hoisted Tipu's standard; *Colonel Gillespie*, with dragoon regiment of *Arcot*, quelled them, killing many.—*Lord Minto*, however, gave them "*genteel*" treatment.

1808. *Ranjit Singh, a Sikh, Raja of all the country west of the Sutlej* (he had commenced as *Raja of Lahore*, district given him by the victorious Afghan, *Zaman Shah*), crossed Sutlej into *territory of Sirhind*, [which was] under British protection, and attacked the *province of the Raja of Patiala*; Minto sent *Colonel Metcalfe* against him. The latter signed first *treaty with Ranjit Singh*, who retired beyond Sutlej, consented to *restore the land he had taken south of that river*, but the *English* were bound not to touch *Sikh territory on north bank of Sutlej*. Ranjit Singh faithfully performed his promises.

1809. *Amir Khan*, now the recognized chief of the *robber tribe of the Pathans*, plundered territories of *Bhonslay*, Raja of Berar, who as an English ally appealed to Minto; but he pushed enemy back over the *Satpura*

Hills before the tardily sent English force arrived at Nagpur.

Second embassy to Persia: embarras de richesse (for animal *fear of Napoleon*) *Sir Harford Jones* was sent *to Teheran* [1808] as ambassador from *London* and *Sir John Malcolm*, from *Calcutta*; their quarrel for precedence, etc. (p. 194). Both were afterwards *superseded* by *Sir Gore Ouseley*, sent from England as *resident ambassador* at Teheran; simultaneously—

Third mission to Kabul, sent by Lord Minto; *Shah Shuja*, brother and successor of *Zaman Shah*, was on throne at that time; the envoy was *Mountstuart Elphinstone*; [he] failed because *Shah Shuja* was overthrown through rebellion; his successor, *Mahmud*, accepted the *protection of the French and the Russians.*

Madras Presidency: here, too, constant alarm because of *France.*—For a while there was in force a réglement under which *commanding officers* had *right of providing tents used by their own regiments*; it was nice source of "gain." Sir *George Barlow*, now President of Madras, roughly did away with this nuisance; he also dismissed *General Macdowall*, the Commander-in-Chief, for *arresting Colonel Munro*, the *Quartermaster-General*, who under *orders of Barlow* had in a report denounced the *tent custom* as *something akin to cheating*, and soon afterwards suspended *four officers of high rank*. All army now in a blaze of mutiny, [and the officers] sent insolent protest to the Governor. Barlow, *calling upon the native soldiers*, soon brought the officers to submit.

1810. *Expedition against Persian Pirates*. From *early 1810* on, there had been a horde of pirates in the Persian Gulf, who were damaging English trade, then seized a ship—*Minerva*—belonging to the Company. Minto sent expedition from Bombay, it captured the pirates' headquarters at *Mallia* (in Gujarat) and, with support from *Imam of Muscat*, stormed and burnt their stronghold at *Shiraz in Persia*, whereby the robbers' "confederation" was broken up.

Expedition to Macao. Under influence of the Company fired with commercial rivalry, *Minto* sent ship to *Macao* to destroy the *Portuguese settlement* there, which was under protection of the Emperor of China; the regiment sent thither came back to Bengal without success; *Emperor of China at once abolished English trade at Macao.*

Seizure of Mauritius and Bourbon.—During the French war with England, the *Company's trade* had suffered a great deal *from French attacks on the islands of Mauritius and Bourbon.* To put an end to this, Minto sent *expedition under command of Colonel Keating*, who first took *Isle of Rodrigues*, 200 miles from Mauritius.

May 1810, he made Rodrigues his base of operations; first *attack on Isle of Bourbon*, troops landed, *attacked city and harbour of St. Paul*, four batteries stormed, *the place taken* after three hours' fighting; *the enemy's fleet*, blocka ded by the English one, *surrendered.*

July. After several other *French stations* had been taken in Isle of *Bourbon*, the *capital*, *Saint-Denis*, fell, and the *whole French force surrendered. Colonel Willoughby* was left in command, the arsenal was turned into an English storehouse, where preparations were made for attack on *Mauritius*, alias *Île de France.*— At sea, *11 English ships taken by the French.*

October 29, 1810, *expedition against Mauritius* landed 1,000 men there; on *October 30*,[1] the French commander *surrendered Mauritius*; *English* have *kept* it till now, but *Isle of Bourbon* was restored to *the French* in *1814.*

1811. *Minto sent expedition against Java.* First to be taken was *spice island of Amboina*, where in *1623* the *terrible massacre by the Dutch* had taken place; soon after, *five smaller Molucca isles* were taken; soon after, *Banda Neira* was taken (ditto Molucca isle). (*The whole expedition* was *due to the East India Co.'s greedy eye on Dutch trade.*)

August 4, 1811. *English landed during night at Batavia* (*capital of Java*). Dutch force concentrated for defence in *Fort Cornelis.*

August 5, *action*, and reduction of *Batavia, by Colonel Gillespie.* Soon afterwards, Sir *Samuel Auchmuty*, commander of the expedition, took *all strong places*

[1] December 9, according to Burgess.

of Java; French and Dutch submitted; Sir *Stamford Raffles* was appointed *Governor of Java.*

Rise of the Pindaris: mounted robbers, thieves by profession. (*Pindaris—mountaineers, peuplade*[1] *in Malwa,* in the états[2] of *Holkar, Sindhia, and Bhopal*—Vindhya Hills=ramas[3] of robbers, escaped criminals, déserteurs, aventuriers; they first appeared in *1761, during battle at Panipat, on the Maratha side.*) *Under Peshwa Baji Rao,* they always emerged *on the side which paid best.*

1808. *Two brothers, Heran and Baran,* headed them as leaders; on their death, a *Jat* named *Chitu* took the command, and styled himself Raja; for his assistance, Sindhia gave him a *small tract of country,* and in same way *other Pindari chiefs* became *possessors of small jagirs; two years later,* Chitu joined *Amir Khan* the Rohilla, and with army of 60,000 they began *plundering Central India.* Lord Minto was refused permission to attack them by the *Board of Control,* whose refusal was based on *Cornwallis' doctrine of non-intervention.*

Ryotwari System in Madras, established by *Sir Thomas Munro;* first recognized as *basis of the revenue administration of the Madras Presidency; not permanently ordained till 1820.* It functioned as follows: *Revenue officers of the Government* made an *annual settlement early in year,* when crops were sufficiently advanced to judge of their abundance and quality; at this time, the *government tax equalled one-third of the produce;* the *cultivator* was held responsible for this tax, as assessed and inscribed in the *pottah,* or *lease, annually granted* to him. If *failure occurred owing to accidents of climate, the whole village was ordered to be ratably assessed, to bear the burden of the tax upon the land which had failed;* if *such a failure* [was believed to have come about] *by the wilful obstinacy of a ryot* who, after having accepted the *pottah,* refused *to cultivate his land,* the *collector had power*

[1] Tribe.
[2] Possessions.
[3] Gangs.

to punish him by fine or even by *corporal chastisement.* The collector, with his absolute power *to withhold or grant the pottah,* had during each year *absolute control over each district.*

October 1813. *Lord Minto* went back to England; [appointed] in his place [was] the *Marquis of Hastings,* then *called Earl of Moira.*

Proceedings in Parliament. **March 1, 1813,** *charter of the East India Co.* expired again.

March 22, 1813. *House of Commons resolved itself into a committee* to consider the questions in detail. The *Board of Directors at the India House* pleaded that the conquered country belonged by right to the *Company,* not to the *Crown*; their [the Company's] *monopoly* [of trade] was ditto necessary; they claimed new *charter again for a period of 20 years,* on same basis as the previous one.—The *President of the Board of Commissioners, Earl of Buckinghamshire,* opposed all these arguments. *India* belonged to *England,* not to the Company, [he said]; *free Indian trade for all British subjects* and *down with the monopoly of the Company*; in fact, it would be better if *the Crown* were to take *government of India completely into its hands.*

March 23, *Lord Castlereagh* moved *on behalf of the Ministry: charter of the Company to be extended for 20 years; Company to have monopoly in Chinese trade,* but *Indian trade to be thrown open* to the world on *certain restrictions,* preventing injury to the Company; Company to retain *command of the army and power of appointing their own civil and other servants.*

Late July, *this*—Castlereagh's—*bill* was *passed* with very slight alterations (see *p. 200* for more). *Lord Grenville* urged the *Government to take the whole of India absolutely into its hands* and *appoint to the civil service* by open competition.

In the same year, *Christianity* was *openly introduced in India* through *appointment of a bishop to the See of Calcutta.*

. . . .

[XII.] LORD HASTINGS' ADMINISTRATION, 1813-1822

October 1813. *Lord Hastings arrived at Calcutta.*—In *1811*, *Jaswant Rao Holkar* died; his widow, Tulsi Bai, after many other favourites, etc., lived for four years with *Gafur Khan*, chief of the robber Pathans; *government of Indore* [was] fully in his power.—In *1813*, *Sindhia* plundered the country round, [but] desisted on slightest threat of English Government.—The *Rohilla chief, Amir Khan*, [was] at head of one of the best armies in India, consisting of *his own bodies of adventurers* and *the forces of Holkar*, of which *Amir Khan* became Commander-in-Chief in *1811*, after his breach with Pindari chief, *Chitu*.—The *Peshwa, Baji Rao*, was fretting under the English yoke. His position [had become] even "humbler" through energetic conduct of *Mountstuart Elphinstone*, the Resident at his court. There were *disputes with the Gaekwar* over the territory of *Ahmadabad*; in keeping with the treaty, the *English* were called upon to arbitrate. The Gaekwar therefore sent to Poona—and this was approved by Bombay President, *Gangadhar Shastri*; the *latter* was plotted against by the Peshwa's vicious favourite, *Trimbakji Danglia*, who had him cruelly murdered on return to Gujarat by his accomplices—at *Pandharpur*. Despite the Peshwa's resistance, etc. (see p. 202), Elphinstone forced him to deliver *Danglia* to him, and the latter was thrown into *prison* for further inquiry. This was *state of things* at the time of *Hastings'* assumption of government; he found treasury empty.

1814. *The Gurkhas of Nepal*; a race of *Rajputs*; came originally from Rajputana, and conquered and settled in the *tarai*, at the base of the Himalayas, in Nepal. Passing through various changes of government, they [were], in the *middle of the 18th century*, under dominion of one chief styling himself "*Raja of Nepal.*" He extended the boundaries, which sometimes brought him into contact with Ranjit Singh, and sometimes with princes under British protection; hence he already had quarrels with *Sir George Barlow* and *Lord Minto*.—*Late in 1813*, Gurkhas had seized a *district of 200 vil-*

lages under British protection in the annexed territory of Oudh. Lord Hastings demanded their restitution within 25 days; thereupon *the Gurkhas murdered* a British magistrate in *Butwal*. Thereupon—

(October) 1814—*declaration of war against the Gurkhas*: *General Gillespie* was to attack the *Gurkha army*, under command of *Amar Singh, on the Sutlej*; a second division, under *General Wood*, was to march on *Butwal*; a third, under *General Ochterlony*, on *Simla*; *fourth division*, under *General Marley*, was to advance straight on the capital, *Khatmandu*. *A loan of two millions* was obtained from the *Nabob of Oudh* for *the expenses of war*.

October 29. *Gillespie* attacked *Fort of Kalanga*, defended by 500 Gurkhas; he ordered immediate assault, and led it; was *shot himself*; after *loss of 700 officers* and men, division returned to its camp. Command was now assumed by *General Martindale*, who wasted months in useless blockade; after breach had been made and *fort at last captured*, it was [found] already *evacuated*, *its defenders* having, *on the night* previous to the assault, *left it with all their stores*.

General Wood, after victory over a force far inferior to his own, became funky, retreated to British frontier, and remained inactive throughout the rest of the campaign.

1815. *General Marley*, having marched to the frontier, stayed there till early 1815, awaiting battering-train for attack on *Khatmandu*; he broke up his division on march into two feeble parties, *each* was *attacked and defeated by the Gurkhas*; Marley marched to and fro, and on *February 10, 1815, took to his heels all alone across the frontier*!

May 15, after several months of successful engagements and sieges, *Amar Singh* having retired to *Malon* (strong hill-fort on *left bank of Sutlej*), *General Ochterlony* bombarded *Malon* for a month, it *fell on May 15*, *Amar Singh*[1] was *killed during the siege*.—Meanwhile *Almora* had fallen, in district of Kumaon, whereby

[1] Bhakti Singh, Amar Singh's general, according to Mill, Vol. 8.

all supplies were *cut off from the Gurkhas* opposing Ochterlony; they came to terms.

1816. After lengthy negotiations, *fresh campaign.* Sir David Ochterlony effected very difficult passage through the mountains to *Makwanpur*, and repulsed the Gurkhas with heavy loss; he then concluded *treaty with them*, which they kept faithfully; they were bound to their own territory and had *to cede most of the land* conquered by them.—This war opened up communications between England and Nepal; *many Gurkhas* joined the *English army*, were forced into *Gurkha regiments*, of highest service to the English *during the sepoy mutiny of 1857*. The Company's numerous early reverses during the *Gurkha war* occasioned disturbance amongst the native princes, in particular, émeutes in *Hathras* and *Bareili* (both in *Delhi provinces*).

1816-1818. *The Pindaris.* In *1815*, 50,000-60,000 of these freebooters ravaged Central India, while *Amir Khan* threatened the frontier and the *Maratha* princes, in hostile attitude, were collecting armies. *Hastings'* attempts to form, by means of alliances, a strong confederation against *Amir Khan* proved futile (206).

October 14, 1815. A large body of Pindaris attacked and plundered the Nizam's dominions.

February 1816. Nearly half of the Pindari forces invaded the *Guntur Circars* (Company's dominion), made desert of the country, and disappeared before regular attack could be made on them by Madras army.

Raghoji Bhonslay, Raja of Berar, died; succeeded by his cousin *Appa Sahib*, who *murdered Bhonslay's son* and *bought the Company by a treaty* under which *a subsidiary force of 8,000 English* [was to be] *garrisoned in Nagpur.*

November 1816. *New Pindari inroad* into the *Company's territory*; when *Nagpur force took field*, they disappeared into their own country in detached bodies.

1817. *Early in year*, Hastings took field in person, with army of 120,000 men (*largest army* assembled [in India] under British flag). He made *alliances* with the *Rajas of Bundi, Jodhpur, Udaipur, Jaipur and Kotah*, and *Sindhia* was forced to sign a *treaty of neutrality*,

Extinction of the Maratha Powers. Trimbakji Danglia, having slipped away from prison, became again chief adviser of *Baji Rao* at *Poona*; the latter made hostile preparations against English under pretext of "defence against the Pindaris." *Elphinstone* ordered troops from Bombay and told him categorically *to decide for war or peace in 24 hours*, and *to surrender three of his principal fortresses and Trimbakji Danglia*. Baji Rao hesitated; Bombay troops appeared; *Peshwa submitted, gave over all the forts to the Company*, and promised to catch Danglia. Now a *treaty* was *signed*, under which *Peshwa consented never to receive the wakils*[1] *of any other Power, Maratha or foreign, at his court and to remain entirely at the orders of the British Resident*. Thereby *Maratha sovereignty* [became] *extinct, court at Poona* was reduced to the level of that at Nagpur or Indore. Besides, he [the Peshwa] had to cede *Sagar, Bundelkhand*, and other places to the Company. *Elphinstone* then removed for safety to the British camp, two miles [from Poona], and the troops remained stationary there. *About a month later*, Peshwa was caught in the act of raising levies of horsemen and troops to act against the English.

November 5, 1817. With a tolerably large native army encamped close to the British regiments, the (British) *Residency* at Poona was attacked and burnt. In the following action, the *Peshwa's raw levies* were beaten; he himself—*Baji Rao*—

November 17, 1817, *surrendered. End of the sovereignty of the Maratha State* begun in *1669* with *Shivaji*.

Fall of the Raja of Nagpur. Appa Sahib proceeded in same way—levying army, etc.—as Baji Rao; the *British Resident, Mr. Jenkins*, caught him.

September 1817. *Appa Sahib* openly received *a Pindari legate at court*.

November 1817. He informed Jenkins that Peshwa had made him (Appa Sahib) *Commander-in-Chief of the Maratha forces*; Jenkins replied that since Peshwa was

---

[1] Ambassadors.

at war with Company, the appointment would involve Nagpur in a war with the Company. Thereupon *Appa Sahib* attacked (British) *Residency.*—Action in the *Sitabaldi Hills. English won* after bad outset (for them) of the action. *Nagpur occupied*; *Appa Sahib deposed*, died as *fugitive at Jodhpur*. This state administered by the English till *1826*, when they placed *a youth*, who had been nominated, because he had now come of age, on the throne *under British protection*.

Fall of the House of Holkar. Tulsi Bai had made her lover, *Gafur Khan*, chief of the Pathans and an arch-enemy of the Company, the real Governor. *Sir John Malcolm* and *Sir Thomas Hislop* demanded his removal. She—the Rani—prepared war, but one night was seized at Indore by the party hostile to her, beheaded, and her body thrown into the river.

1817. Young *Malhar Rao Holkar* was at once proclaimed sovereign, army marched out, nominally under his leadership, really under that of *Gafur Khan*.

December 21, 1817. English crossed River *Sipra* under terrible fire of the Marathas, and captured their cannons. *Decisive fight at Mahidpur*; *English*, after hard struggle, *victors*. Malhar Rao's sister, *Buna Bai*, captured and sent to her brother.—Soon after, *treaty*: *Malhar Rao Holkar*, son of Jaswant Rao, *acknowledged Raja*, but *his power curtailed* and *his territory reduced*.

Till about end of 1817, the Pindaris had hovered about without coming to decisive action. In view of the fall of the Maratha princes befriended to them, their *three chiefs—Karim Khan, Chitu*, and *Wasil Muhammad*—decided to go about the matter in good earnest; they *concentrated* their troops, which was what Hastings wanted; he ordered *the various armies of the Presidency to close round the robber strongholds in Malwa*, and threw *regular cordon* round them; the three leaders fled, and their *three divisions, which tried to do the same*, were *attacked* [by the British] *while in flight*. Karim Khan's division destroyed by *General Donkin*; *Chitu's force* dispersed by *General Brown*; their *third division* fled in all directions before they were assailed; their chief, *Wasil Muhammad*, committed *suicide*;

Chitu was found dead in a jungle after the battle; *Karim Khan* was permitted to retire and settle on a small estate, on promise of keeping peace. The *Pindaris* were *disbanded*, never again to unite; the *Pathans* under *Amir Khan* and *Gafur Khan* were likewise crushed.

Sindhia now the only *chieftain with an army* or the smallest pretence to independence; but *left completely dependent on the Company.—India now English.*

August 1817. *First outbreak of cholera with terrible vehemence in India*; at first it appeared in *Zillah of Jessore*, near Calcutta, advanced across Asia to *European continent*, which it decimated, from there on *to England*, and *thence to America. In November 1817, the army of Hastings* was attacked by it, the contagion having been brought by *arrival of a new detachment from Calcutta*, and it raged *while Hastings' army was passing through the lowland of Bundelkhand*, and for weeks the track was strewn with dead and dying.

January 1, 1818. Peshwa (he had fled from Poona in southern direction) joined by Trimbakji Danglia. *At head of about 20,000 men*, they *battled against a detachment of English under Captain Staunton*; the latter won after terrible struggle; Marathas were broken, and fled. *General Smith* then assumed command and marched on *Satara*, which surrendered at once. *Baji Rao* fled, surrendered finally to *Sir John Malcolm*, who proclaimed him dethroned. Lord *Hastings* made the *Raja of Satara*, of the actual Maratha rulers (who had been ousted by their ministers, *the peshwas*), *the lineal descendant of Shivaji*, the rightful monarch, the *Peshwa* becoming a *government pensioner*; thus tables turned since *1708*, when *Sahu*, Raja of Satara, had made *Balaji Viswanath* his Peshwa. (*Nana Sahib*, of 1857 insurrection, was *adopted son of Baji Rao, at whose death the annuity paid him by the British Government was stopped.*) Besides, some important forts—*Talneir*, *Maligaon, and Asirgarh*—were captured in that last war show. —*Lord Hastings* proclaimed *liberty of the press* in India.

1819. *Sir Stamford Raffles* obtained *cession of Singapore* from *Tumangoy*, or *Governor*, of *Johore*.

1820. *Nizam* in heavy debts, *owing to the heavy expenses incurred in the maintenance of the Hyderabad contingent* and the scandalous mismanagement of his Minister, *Chander Lal*. The house of *Messrs. Palmer & Co.* eagerly offered him loans at any amount, until the sum owed became hopelessly large. The partners of the Palmer House obtained a very undue influence at Hyderabad; Mr. *Metcalfe*, then Resident there, called upon *Hastings* to interfere; the latter *forbade Palmer & Co. to make more advances*, and directed that *the rents of the Northern Circars* should be at once *capitalized*; the funds so obtained were directed to the payment of the debt. *Palmer & Co. failed* soon after; *Hastings* was damaged by the fact that he had been connected with the House (it was said by friendship with one of its members); that he had *sanctioned many of their previous proceedings of a very questionable character* and interfered only when the matter had, as the result of steps taken by Metcalfe, received a publicity no longer allowing Hastings "to countenance" *the Palmers.*

Late 1822. *Hastings resigned his post. Returned to England on January 1, 1823. He had come to India pledged to a policy of non-annexation!*

. . . .

LAST PERIOD, 1823-1858
(EXTINCTION OF THE EAST INDIA COMPANY)

(1) LORD AMHERST'S ADMINISTRATION, 1823-1828

January 1823. After Hastings' departure, *Mr. Adam*, senior member of the Council, [became Governor-General] per interim.—Board of Control made Lord Amherst Viceroy.

August 1823. *Amherst* in Calcutta; presently involved in *war with the Burmese.—The Burmese of Ava* originally were *mere dependents of the Kingdom of Pegu*; afterwards they became free; at their head [was] *Alompra*, an adventurer, who had always led their armies victoriously; they conquered *Tenasserim* from Siam, defeated the Chinese on several occasions, reduced *all Arakan, subjugated their own feudal superiors at Pegu*, became monarchs of the whole peninsula, with *capital in Ava*. The *King of Burma* styled himself "*Lord of the White Elephants, Monarch of the Sea and the Earth.*"

In 1818, it was already believed at *Court of Ava* that the English, victorious against the prostrate Hindus, would fall before the invincible Burmese, and their King wrote to Calcutta, demanding from *East India Co.* the *cession of Chittagong* and *certain other districts* because, he said, these were parts of the *territory of Arakan* belonging to him. However, he kept quiet on receiving *Hastings*' courteous reply as to his "error."

1822. The Burmese troops, under their *Maha Bandula* (Commander-in-Chief), *conquered and annexed Assam*.

1823. They *seized* the English island of *Shahpuri*, on the *coast of Arakan*, and slaughtered the little garrison there. *Amherst* sent a force to dislodge the Burmese, wrote courteously to King at Ava, asking him to punish the offenders, whom he treated as mere *pirates*.

January 1824. The Burmese, seeing therein sign of weakness, invaded province of *Kachar*, [which was] under British protection; English troops defeated them and drove them to *Manipur*.—Two expeditions were now sent from Calcutta, one to take *Assam*, the other to capture *Rangoon* and *the other seaports of Burma*.

1824. *Rangoon* taken without a blow, garrison fleeing into the interior. *Sir Archibald Campbell*, the commander of this expedition, took ditto a few neighbouring entrenchments and, after prolonged resistance, *Kemmendine* (four miles from Rangoon); then, because of hot weather, his troops were placed in cantonments at Rangoon; *failing provisions*, *outbreak of cholera* among his troops.

December 1824. *Maha Bandula*, with 60,000 men, came down on Campbell's army; English defeated him twice; he retreated to *Donabyu*, followed by the English, who closely besieged the town.

April 1825. *Maha Bandula killed* by a rocket, the *garrison of Donabyu surrendered*. Campbell pushed on, took the city of *Prome* (alias *Pri*) without firing a shot; rested here, awaiting the result of the expedition of *Assam*; the force sent thither under *Colonel Richards* took *Rangpur* and *Sylhet*, expelled the Burmese from Assam and, under General Macbean's command, advanced—

March 1825—into *Arakan*, where it passed through the bravely defended hills; English, victorious, debouched into the plains, and appeared before *capital of Arakan*. Negotiations with Ava Court led to nothing.

November 1825. Campbell marched forth on *Ava*; enemy fled before him.

February 1826. *Two decisive actions*, Burmese defeated; English reached *Yandabo*, two days' march from Ava; *Burmese King submitted*.

1826. *Treaty with Burma*: King of Burma *ceded Assam*, *Yeh* (a province of Tenasserim), *Tenasserim, and part of the Arakan, to the Company*; promised *non-inter-*

ference with province of Kachar, to pay *£1 million* for war expenses, and to receive a *British Resident* at Ava.

This first Burmese war (*1824-1826*) cost the British Government £13 million; was unpopular in England.

October 1824 (during the war), *47th Bengal Native Infantry*, quartered at *Barrackpore*, under orders to Rangoon, broke out in open mutiny (cf. p. 218).

1826. *At the end of the war, another mutiny* at the same place (cf. p. 218).

January 18, 1826. Army under *Lord Combermere* stormed *Bharatpur, considered* impregnable. This *State of Bharatpur* was founded by the *Jats*, the aboriginal inhabitants of the country, *at the time of the disintegration of the Mogul Empire*. At that time [1826] it was ruled by *Durjan Sal*; the latter had wrested the "kingdom" from the rightful heir, Baldeo Singh (infant), whose supporters called on the English for aid; hence Combermere was sent against him, etc. After the fall of Bharatpur, *Durjan Sal* was sent to Benares as British prisoner and Baldeo Singh installed as Raja under British protection.

1827. *Amherst* received *thanks from Parliament for Burmese war*, was created Earl, and returned to England in *February 1828*.

. . . .

(2) LORD WILLIAM BENTINCK'S ADMINISTRATION, 1828-1835

(*Cf. p. 219 for selection of Bentinck against Company's wishes.*)

July 4, 1828. *Bentinck in Calcutta.*—In the *Rajput State of Jodhpur, the Raja, Man Singh*, was *reinstated by the English* against the will of his rebel chieftains.

Gwalior, **1827.** *Daulat Rao Sindhia died* without issue or adopted son. Bentinck ordered his wife—the Rani—to *adopt a son*, she chose the nearest male relative, *Ali Jah Jankoji Sindhia*, and in *1833* the latter engaged in warfare with the *Rani*; she was ordered by

Bentinck *completely* to transfer the *government* to him.

At *Jaipur*, the Vizier had poisoned the Raja and his mother, the Rani, and seized government. The British *Resident* interfered; placed on throne an *infant*, the only representative of the royal family. The Resident assumed charge of the country during his minority.

Oudh, **1834.** Mr. *Maddock* inquired into the maladministration of the *Raja of Oudh*, who devoured all revenues; the Raja received *severe warning* from Governor-General.

Bhopal, **1820.** *Raja of Bhopal* died, his widow, *Sikandar Begum*, was left to govern the country; the rightful heir, her nephew, having appealed to British Government in *1835*, Bentinck interfered, *placed him on the throne* (reigning now is *Begum*, daughter of this Raja).

Kurg, **1834.** Bentinck annexed *Kurg* (southern Malabar coast). In *1820*, *Vira Raja* had succeeded, and begun by wholesale slaughter of his relatives. In *1834*, *Vira Raja* declared war to the Company, Madras army occupied his capital, he renounced everything; [the state] *annexed* because there was no other royal prince.

Kachar. *Annexed in 1830*; was *under British protection* during the Burmese war; but in *1830 Raja Govind Chandra died* heirless.

Mysore, **1811.** The young Raja (of the *ancient* royal family, whom *Wellesley* had reinstated on the throne of Mysore in *1799*—as infant of five years—under *Purnaiya's* direction during his minority) came of age, dismissed Purnaiya, wasted treasury, ran into debt, cruelly oppressed the ryots, so that, in *1830*, *half the raj in a state of insurrection*; British force quelled the rising; *Bentinck annexed Mysore*; the Raja was pensioned with *annuity of £ 40,000* and *one-fifth of the revenues of the country*; the increase of the revenues had made this latter "bit" exceedingly valuable. (Thus, in their pensioning off—at their annexations—the English burdened the poor Hindus in favour of the dispossessed princes and princelings.)

Insurrections—among the wild tribes of the *Kolis*, *Dhangars*, and *Santals* in the south-west of Bengal, in the territories of *Ramghur*, *Palamau*, and *Chhota Nagpur*, and among the *Choars* in country near *Bankura*—quelled with much slaughter.—Also, *formidable disturbance at Barasat, near Calcutta*, where bloody fight broke out between Moslem fanatics under *Titu Mir* and Hindus. *British regiment* put the rioters down.

1827. Lord Amherst's flirting with *Ranjit Singh* (the "*Lion*
Sikhs *of Lahore*"); ditto of *Lord Bentinck in 1831* (*durbar on the Sutlej*) (cf. p. 222).

1832. *Commercial treaty with the amirs of Sind*, under which *the Sutlej and the Indus* were *opened for traffic* for the first time, with co-operation of Ranjit Singh.

Quarrel between Bentinck and officers *at Calcutta*, because of reducing bonus from "*single*" ro "*half-batta*" (p. 223). *Abolition of suttee* (l. c.). *Law reforms, abolition of thuggee* (p. 224).—*Law and justice* (223-224). In *1835*, *Bentinck* founded a *Medical College* for the natives at *Calcutta*.

1833. *North-Western Provinces* created a *separate presidency*; gave them a new [*Supreme*] *Court* and *Board of Revenues at Allahabad*. *Land settlement of these provinces for 30 years* (framer and controller of this work, *Robert Bird*.)

Peninsular and Oriental Company, opening up steam communication by way of Red Sea, brought India two months nearer to England; the Company, established in *1842*, received *support* from home and Calcutta governments.

1833. (*Parliamentary Proceedings*.) Charter had expired again, old debates were resumed over *same points*, but [this time] free trade party was in ascendancy. *Trade with China* was *opened to all traders*; *last* of *the Company's trade monopoly* against private trade was thus swept away.—The new, *fourth presidency*—the North-Western Provinces—created by *Act of Parliament*.—*Another Act* gave *Governor-General* in *Council increased power of interference with the local governments of the several provinces*; *the local governors were to have no councils* and *no powers of legislation*. *Governor-General* to legislate for all persons, European or native, and for all courts. *Commission appointed* to inquire into possibility of *a single code of laws for all India*.

. . . .

(3) SIR CHARLES METCALFE, PROVISIONARY GOVERNOR-GENERAL, 1835-1836

He had been *Governor of Agra*, named per interim. *Court of Directors* wanted Parliament to make him definitely *Governor-General*, but *Ministry* wanted *absolutely* to keep appointment in their hands; they conferred the post on Lord *Heytesbury*, but before he started, the Tories were displaced by *Whigs*; and their *new President of the Board of Control*, *Sir John Hobhouse*, revoked Heytesbury's appointment, and nominated *Lord Auckland*.

1835. *Metcalfe proclaimed liberty of the press in India.* The enraged *Directors* of the *India House* at London (the *Court*) treated him, one of the best Indian functionaries, so rudely that he resigned his post in *civil service on Auckland's arrival*, and returned to England.

. . . .

(4) LORD AUCKLAND'S ADMINISTRATION, 1836-1842

March 20, 1836. *Auckland* assumed government in Calcutta. He *began the Afghan war* (under Palmerston's inspiration).

Afghan dynasties. In 1757, *Ahmad Shah Durani* conquered *Delhi*; *in 1761*, [he] fought the terrible *Battle of Panipat* against the Marathas. (He was chieftain of the *Afghan tribe of the Abdalis or Duranis.*) In *1761*, back in Afghanistan, *Ahmad Shah Durani* reigned *in Kabul.*[1] On his death (*1773*), he was succeeded by his son Timur Shah (*1773-1792*[2]); under him, the family of *Barakzais* rose, whose head, *Payandah Khan*, [was] Vizier of the weak Timur; this last in a fit of rage mortally offended the *Barakzais*; they *raised insurrection*, whereupon Timur captured and killed *Payandah Khan*; the *Barakzais* swore vendetta on the *Sadozais* (as

[1] The book used by Marx is in error on this point, for Ahmad Shah ruled and died in Kandahar.

[2] 1793, according to *The Cambridge History of India*, Vol. 5, 1929.

the royal family were called);[1] throne went to *Timur's son*—

1792-1802—*Zaman Shah.* He annoyed *the Company* a great deal by war demonstrations on the Indian border; his *intentions with regard to Hindustan* frustrated by the *Barakzais* and his *own brothers*, of whom four played [a certain] role: *Shuja-ul-Mulk*, *Mahmud*, *Firuz*, and *Kaisar*.—*Payandah Khan* was followed in *headship of the Barakzai clan* by his son, *Fateh Khan*.

1801, when Zaman [Shah] was at *Peshawar*, upon great expedition on his way to Hindustan, *Fateh Khan* won over Zaman's brother *Mahmud* to conspire with him, raised his standard, and seized *Kandahar*; *Zaman* hurried back, was *captured*, *blinded*, *imprisoned*, *lived for a long time* as miserable dependent. *Shuja-ul-Mulk*, rightful successor, marched at once on Kabul, but Fateh defeated him, and placed on throne—

1802[2]-1818—*Mahmud Shah*, while *Firuz* seized on the *Sadozai dominions of Herat* and *Kaisar*, *on those of Kandahar*.

1808.[3] At instigation of many of the Durani nobles at Kabul, *Shah Shuja* returned, defeated the usurpers, pardoned all, left his brothers as governors of Herat and Kandahar. *Fateh Khan* fled, *plotted first with Kaisar* and in the latter's name raised *new revolt*, was beaten, *Kaisar* pardoned.—*Fateh Khan* then made rebellion in name of *Kamran*, Shah Mahmud's eldest son, and treacherously took *Kandahar* from Kaisar. Revolt quelled again, and once more *Shah Shuja* pardoned the rebels.—Fateh Khan persuaded *Kaisar* to head a rebellion, they seized Peshawar, rebels again defeated, again forgiven.—New rebellion by *Fateh Khan*, this time victorious, *Shah Shuja* compelled to flee [in 1810]; caught in *Kashmir*, whose Governor tried

[1] The book used by Marx is in error on this point. Payandah Khan placed Zaman on the throne after Timur's death, and was murdered by Zaman, who wanted to get rid of too influential a vizier. It was then that enmity flared up between the Barakzais and Sadozais. See *History of the Afghans* by Ferrier, *The Cambridge History of India*, Vol. 5, etc.

[2] 1800, according to Burgess.

[3] 1803, according to Burgess.

to extort the *Koh-i-noor diamond* from him; Shuja fled to *Ranjit Singh* in *Lahore*, who at first pretended friendship and then mistreated him, and grabbed the Koh-i-noor *diamond*; *Shuja* slipped away to *Ludhiana*, where he found a new friend in *Raja Kistawar*. Shuja launched ineffectual attack on *Kashmir*, and returned to Ludhiana.

1816. *Mahmud Shah* weak and inept ruler; all real power in hands of *Fateh Khan and the Barakzais.—Dost Mohammed*, a younger *brother of Fateh Khan*, planned with him to raise the Barakzais to the throne, but first they wanted to bring *all Afghanistan* under one man; they marched on *Herat* (governed by *Firuz*); Herat was seized by them and *Firuz* fled, while his nephew, *Prince Kamran*, swore vengeance on the Barakzais, particularly Fateh Khan; he went to *Kabul*, persuaded his half-imbecile father, *Shah Mahmud*, that *Fateh Khan's* movement was insurrection, obtained his permission to seize the latter and bring him to Kabul; did so; *in presence of Mahmud and his son Kamran, Fateh Khan* was *butchered* in the most cannibalistic manner (cf. p. 230). Then *Dost Mohammed* came up with large army, *all Barakzais* supporting him, *took Kabul*, sent Mahmud and Kamran into exile; they fled to *Firuz* in Herat.—The *Barakzais* seized the Kingdom of Afghanistan. Besides *Dost Mohammed*, Fateh Khan had the following brothers: *Mohammed*, who seized *Peshawar*; *Azim Khan* (the eldest brother), who marched on *Kabul*, claiming it as head of the family of Dost Mohammed; while *Pur Dil Khan*, *Kohan Dil Khan*, and *Sher Ali Khan* seized on *Kandahar* and the *country of the Khiljies*. Dost Mohammed surrendered *Kabul* to *Azim Khan* and withdrew to *Ghazni.—Azim Khan* set up a puppet sovereign, *Prince Ayub*, a representative of the ancient *Sadozai* Dynasty, as nominal Shah at Kabul; but *Dost Mohammed* set up another representative [of the same dynasty], *Sultan Ali*, who was killed by *Ayub*. Soon after, when *Dost Mohammed and Azim Khan* had launched an expedition against the *Sikhs*, Azim Khan learnt that *his brother Dost* was leagued against him with

Ranjit Singh, fled in terror to *Jalalabad*, where he died in 1823; Ranjit Singh gave *Dost Mohammed Peshawar*, and Dost became actual head of Afghanistan; the *Kandahar Barakzais* seized *Kabul* in a moment of confusion, and it was not until—

1826—that *Dost Mohammed* [became] *master of Kabul* by driving out the other claimants. He reigned well and with moderation, sought as much as possible to crush *the Durani tribes.*

1834. *Shah Shuja*, raising army in *Sind*, made new attempt to regain his kingdom, had *co-operation* of various brothers of Dost, who were jealous of the latter.

1834. *Shuja* did not obtain from Lord Bentinck the support he had hoped for, and *Ranjit Singh* offered his own at so high a price that Shuja refused it; *Shuja* marched into Afghanistan, *invested Kandahar*, but city defended itself bravely; *Dost Mohammed* moved up with army from Kabul in the rear of *Shuja*, who, after one feeble battle, fled back to India.—*Ranjit Singh* on this occasion *annexed Peshawar*; *Dost Mohammed* proclaimed a *religious war against the Sikhs*, marched with enormous army *into the Punjab*; but his expedition was frustrated by *General Harlan*, an *American in the pay of Ranjit Singh*, entering the *Afghan camp* as an ambassador and intriguing there so well that army was disaffected, half of it broke up and marched off again by different routes; *Dost* returned to Kabul.

1837.[1] *Ranjit Singh* took *Kashmir* and *Multan*; Dost's son, *Akbar Khan*, distinguished himself in the unsuccessful expedition against him.

Persia. Agha Mohammad and his [nephew] *Fateh Ali* had raised Persia as *successive shahs. Fateh Ali* had two sons: *Abbas Mirza* the *Shah Zada* and *Mohammad.*

1834.[2] *Abbas Mirza* prevailed upon old *Fateh Ali* to undertake expedition to *Herat*, but *Fateh* died that year [1834]; *Abbas Mirza* [killed]; *Mohammad* acceded to throne and, under inspiration of *Count Simonich*, the

---

[1] According to *The Cambridge History of India*, Vol. 5, Kashmir was taken in 1819 and Multan, in 1818.

[2] 1833, according to Sykes, *A History of Persia*, Vol. 2, London, 1921.

Russian Ambassador at *Teheran*, undertook, *against wish of the English*—

1837—*siege of Herat*. Pretext: some tribute, asked by *Mohammad Shah* and refused by *Kamran*, now called *Shah of Herat*.

September 1838. *Persians withdrew*, nominally *at the request of the English*, in fact because they could not do anything against the *Afghan garrison of Herat*. One *Eldred Pottinger*, then a young lieutenant still, distinguished himself in the garrison of Herat during the siege.

1836. The British Minister at the Court of Persia warned *Auckland* of the *Persian expedition to Herat*, describing it as Russian manoeuvre, etc.; therefore—

1837—*Auckland* sent *Captain Alexander Burnes* to *Kabul* to secure *commercial treaty* and more intimate relations with Afghanistan: [Burnes] found on his arrival that the *Kandahar chiefs* had asked Russian aid against *Ranjit Singh* and that (!?) Dost Mohammed *seemed* inclined to follow their example. During *Burnes*'s *residence at Kabul*, the *Barakzais* actually made *a treaty with Persia under Russian dictation*; and *Mr. McNeill*, the *English Ambassador at Teheran*, was treated with "indignity." Burnes's mission a failure, *Dost Mohammed* demanding that whichever party he treated with should *procure him Peshawar from Ranjit Singh*. The Russian Ambassador promised it; *Burnes* was unable to do so; thereupon *Dost Mohammed* declared for Russia, and *Burnes* left Afghanistan.

June 26, 1838. *Lahore tripartite• treaty* between *Lord Auckland*, *Ranjit Singh*, and *Shah Shuja*; the latter absolutely to renounce *Peshawar* and the *states on the Indus in favour of Ranjit Singh*; between Afghans and Sikhs, mutual support; *Shuja to be replaced on throne of Afghanistan*, to relinquish *all claims on Sind* for *payment to be fixed by Governor-General*; to leave *Herat* untouched in hands of *his nephew Kamran*; to *prevent all other foreigners from invasion of British or Sikh territory*.

October 1, 1838. *Simla Proclamation* by Auckland of *war against Afghanistan* for the restoration of the English ally, *Shuja*, to throne. *Futile opposition in British Parliament*, baffled by *Pam*,[1] the real instigator of the whole *farce, avowedly "anti-Russian."* (Pam had in the meantime—"*to overawe Persia,*" while he was in most intimate relation with the Russian, Simonich, at Teheran Court—seized the *island of Karrak*, in the *Persian Gulf*). *Council of war* held under *Auckland*'s auspices: *main* [English] *army* to join *Ranjit Singh*'s *force* at *Firuzpur*; the *Bombay contingent* sailed to the *mouth of the Indus*; the three divisions to meet at *Shikarpur* in *Sind* and to march *jointly to Afghanistan. Co-operation of the amirs of Sind* required to this end.

1786. These *amirs—Baluchis, chieftains of the Talpura tribe*—had conquered *Sind* from the Afghans, portioned out the country among themselves, and established *feudal system.*

1831. (When on way to the Court of Ranjit Singh with his troop of dray horses [intended as a gift]) *Captain Burnes* had treated with the *amirs*, and in 1832, *Lord William Bentinck* had concluded a *formal treaty* with them, whereby the *trade of the Indus* was opened for British merchants.

1835. *Ranjit Singh* commenced a war with the amirs, but (*East India*) *Company* made him desist.

1838. The *tripartite treaty* ensured the amirs of Sind peaceable possession [of their lands] on condition of *payment*, to be fixed by Governor-General, to be made to Shah Shuja.

Early 1839, *Pottinger* was sent [to Sind] to *demand a large payment of the amirs* under the absurdly shameless pretext of *feudal tribute* owed by the amirs to *Shuja* as *Shah of Afghanistan*. They pleaded: Shuja, while in exile, had granted them a *release from that tribute* for an *immediate* payment they had made for him in 1833, [but] *Pottinger* insisted on the "*funds,*" saying that otherwise they [the amirs] would be displaced; *they paid* with just rage.

November 1838. *Bengal* army reached the *Sutlej*, the force of Ranjit Singh joined them there.

---

[1] Palmerston.

December 10, 1838. The *united armies* under command of *Sir Willoughby Cotton* marched from *Firuzpur*, en route for the rendezvous at *Shikarpur* (in *Sind*), (after the Commander-in-Chief, *Sir Henry Fane, had resigned in indignation at the whole proceedings*); they reached—

January 14, 1839—*Sind territory*, and heard that *Sir John Keane* had safely arrived at *Tatta* with his troops from Bombay.

January 29, 1839. *Sir Alexander Burnes* was sent to demand *from the amirs* (of Sind) *cession of the fort of Bakar*, on the Indus, as *depot for the British troops*. They were compelled to do so. *Army* pushed on along the *left* (eastern) *bank of the Indus* to *Hyderabad*; simultaneously the *Bombay contingent* marched along the right bank and halted opposite Hyderabad, and *Karachi* was taken by a British ship with some reserve forces on board, who turned the city into an *English fort*. The amirs submitted in everything to the Company, and the main army marched to *Shikarpur*, where they *arrived*—

At end of February 1839; without *awaiting the Bombay contingent under Sir John Keane* and *Shah Shuja* accompanying him, *Sir Willoughby Cotton* pushed on to *Bolan Pass*; he had to cross a *parched desert 146 miles* in extent, suffered, baggage-animals dying by scores.

March 10, 1839, the column reached *Dadar*, at the mouth of the pass; *Cotton* rested a few days, found that *Mehrab Khan*, of *Khelat*, was hostile; no supplies to be obtained.

March 1839. *Bolan Pass traversed* without opposition in six days; *Cotton halted at Quetta* to await Sir John Keane's arrival; made favourable treaty with *Mehrab Khan*.

April 1839. *Sir john Keane* with his staff joined at *Quetta*, where the whole expedition was now massed, with *Shah Shuja* in camp. Much privation and sickness on further march, the allies soon reached *Kandahar*, which surrendered without fighting.

Early in May 1839, *Shuja* was crowned *Shah of Afghanistan at Kandahar*.

Late in June 1839, army marched to *Ghazni*; strong fort, but its gates were blown down by engineers under Captain Thompson, and in one morning the *city was carried and garrison put to flight. Dost Mohammed* fled to *Hindu Kush* from Kabul, against which the English were marching; they took it without fighting, and—

August 7—*Shah Shuja* was installed at Kabul, in his fathers' *palace* at the immensely strong *Bala Hissar. Shuja's son*, Prince *Timur*, and a *fresh Sikh contingent* came through Khyber Pass, joined soon after the *main army at Kabul.*

(June 27, *Ranjit Singh died*; had left his Sikh kingdom to his eldest son, *Kharak Singh*, and *bequeathed Koh-i-noor to the temple of Jagannath.*) It was decided for the present to leave *large British force and the Sikhs* in *Kabul*, where they remained undisturbed *from 1839 to 1841*; they felt so safe that *Sir William Macnaghten*, the political agent, had his wife and daughter come to Kabul from Hindustan, and other ladies closely related to the officers in the army, because of the *pleasant fresh climate* of Afghanistan.

October 15, 1839. On its southward march back to Sind, the *Bombay force* took *Khelat*, *killed Mehrab Khan*, and *ravaged his country.*

Early 1840, *Macnaghten and Cotton* were such asses that they ceded the immense stronghold of *Bala Hissar* at Kabul to *Shah Shuja* for *his harem* (!) *removing the troops from there into cantonments*. Thus the *strongest fort in the country was converted into a zenana.* Then began a *series of revolts against Shah Shuja* in Kabul itself; it lasted throughout *1840.*

November 1840. *Dost Mohammed*, with a small troop of horsemen, came to Kabul to surrender.—(He had earlier fled to Bokhara, where he was accorded a poor reception, and had returned to Afganistan, was joined by a large number of *Uzbeks and Afghans*, defeated, and put to flight by Brigadier Dennie.)

During remainder of 1840 and summer of 1841, *serious insurrections at Kandahar*, put down severely; *people of Herat openly declared against the British.* The whole country roused to indignation against the "*British usurpers.*"

October 1841, *most serious revolt among the Khilji tribes of the great Khyber Pass*; cost many lives to the troops returning through that pass to Hindustan; suppressed with difficulty.

November 2, 1841. After secret conspiracy organized at Kabul, *house of Burnes* attacked by insurgents, he himself with numerous other officers *foully murdered.* Several regiments sent to quell the insurrection, but *blocked* by mistake in the narrow streets of Kabul; for several days the frantic mob thus left unopposed; they *attacked a fort used for commissariat stores* and so poorly supported by *General Elphinstone* (now *Commander-in-Chief* in Afghanistan *in place of Cotton*) that the officer in charge with his small garrison was forced to clear the fort.—*Macnaghten* sent urgent messages to *General Sale*, then near the Khyber Pass, and to *General Nott* at *Kandahar* to relieve the garrison at Kabul, but *snow* lying thick on ground made any communication hopeless; *troops were in two divisions*, one at the *Bala Hissar* under able *Brigadier Shelton*, the other in cantonments under *General Elphinstone*. Nothing was done because of quarrels between the two.

November 1841, *Afghans* commenced regular attacks, seized *some hills near*; ineffectual attempts to dislodge them.

November 23, 1841. *General action, English completely beaten*, returned to cantonments; *negotiations* in vain; a a few days later, *Akbar Khan*, Dost's fiery son, arrived [in Kabul].

December 11, 1841. *Provisions ran out*; with one voice the inhabitants of the country round refused to supply them; *Macnaghten* had to conclude a *treaty with the insurgents*: *British and Sikh troops to quit the country*; *Dost Mohammed to be released*; *Shah Shuja* to reside *crownless*, but unmolested, in Afghanistan or India; *Afghans guaranteed to assist the safe retreat of the British army by money, protection, and provisions.* Thereupon the *15,000 British troops* began their miserable *retreat from Afghanistan*; the *Afghans* on every occasion *despoiled* (quite so!) *the soldiers* and *seized their stores*;

before the troops had started from Kabul, *Akbar Khan* sent in fresh treaty to *Macnaghten*, invited him to *private audience.*

December 23, 1841. *Macnaghten accepted*, to secure better terms for the army; *Akbar put a pistol shot through his heart.*

January 1842. *Major Pottinger* stepped in Macnaghten's place; was unable to urge some decided course on the despairing generals; made a *final treaty* for securing a safe retreat to the army, left Kabul, but *Akbar Khan* had sworn the annihilation of the British. The troops had scarcely left cantonments when heavy snow came; the soldiers' suffering terrible; *after three days' march, the head of the column entered a pass in the mountains*; *Akbar Khan* appeared with troop of horse, demanded *surrender of all the ladies and children* (including Lady Macnaghten and Lady Sale) with several officers, as *hostages for the safe retreat of the force*; they were given up. *In the defile, the natives* shot the "British dogs" dead from the *heights above*, hundreds fell thus until the *end of the pass was cleared*, where only *500-600* starving and wounded men were left to continue their retreat. They, too, were *slaughtered like sheep* during their struggling march to the frontier.

January 13, 1842. On the *walls of Jalalabad* (near *Shahjahanpur*, North-Western Provinces), the sentries espied a *man in a tattered English uniform*, on miserable pony, horse and man desperately wounded; it was *Dr. Brydon*, the *sole survivor of the 15,000* who had left Kabul three weeks before. He was dying of starvation.

Lord Auckland ordered *the advance of a fresh brigade*, to relieve the *brigade of General Sale* in *Jalalabad, harassed by the Afghans.* Auckland returned disgraced to England; he was succeeded by the big-mouthed elephant, *Lord Ellenborough*, who was sent out *pledged to a peace policy*, but during *the two years of his office*, the sword was *never sheathed* (duce[1] Pam).

. . . .

[1] Led by.

(5) LORD ELLENBOROUGH'S (ELEPHANT'S) ADMINISTRATION, 1842-1844

Early 1842. *On landing*, the "*Elephant*" heard that the *brigade* under *General Wild, sent off by Auckland* to relieve *Jalalabad*, had been *disastrously beaten in Khyber Pass*; that *Sikh army* refused to co-operate any longer with English and that the *sepoys* in Wild's brigade were likewise in a state of panic.

> On his *death* (*June 27, 1839*), *Ranjit Singh* was succeeded by his eldest son, *Kharak Singh*, as ruler of the Punjab; the latter made one *Chait Singh* his Vizier; he was murdered by *ex-Vizier Dian Singh*, who also deposed *Kharak* and replaced him by his son, *Nao Nihal*.
>
> In *1840*, *Kharak Singh* died in prison, and *Nao Nihal* was accidentally killed; *Dian* sent for *Sher Singh*, *Ranjit Singh's* brave son, who seemed to declare for the English.

1842. New brigade under *General Pollock* was sent in assistance of *Wild*; with the liberated Wild it had to penetrate *Khyber Pass* and replace *General Sale* at *Jalalabad*.

April 5, 1842. *Pollock* had two brigades scale the heights on both sides of (*Khyber*) *Pass*, so as to clear the way for advance of the main body; it was done; the *Khyberis, defeated on their own ground*, fled to the Afghan end of the defile. Army marched through pass *unopposed*, reached *Jalalabad in 10 days* (April 15?), where they learnt that siege of the city under *Akbar Khan's* personal command [had been] beaten off in sortie and that *Akbar Khan* had retired.

> *In January* 1842, *General Nott* had concentrated his small force at *Kandahar*, defeated the Afghans on several occasions; afterwards he was *besieged*, defended the city with great ability; but *Ghazni* had *surrendered* to the enemy, and *General England*, commanding a convoy from *Quetta*, *intended to join Nott's force*, had been repulsed and forced to retreat.

Elephant Ellenborough—now singing small—ordered Pollock to *remain* at *Jalalabad till October* and then to withdraw altogether from Afghanistan; *Nott* was also to *destroy Kandahar* and then retire *to the Indus.*—*Cry of rage among all Anglo-Indians*; hence—

July 1842—*the Elephant permitted the military in Afghanistan* to take *Kabul.*—At *Kabul*, *Akbar Khan* had installed himself as *Shah of Afghanistan*, *Shah Shuja* having been barbarously murdered after the retreat of the English. *Akbar* sent the *English ladies*, officers, and other prisoners to a *fort at Tegeen*, where they were well treated. There *General Elphinstone died.*

August 1842. The *two armies of Kandahar and Jalalabad* marched in different directions on Kabul, *Pollock* beating the *Khiljies* several times.

September 1842. The two divisions *joined at Tegeen* (*Tezin*, near *Jalalabad*); *Akbar Khan defeated.*

September 15, 1842. *Kabul in English hands again.*—As *Pollock* advanced, the *British prisoners* were sent to *Bamian* in *Hindu Kush*, in charge of officer *Sala Mohammed*; the latter, hearing of defeat of Akbar, offered Pottinger to release the whole party and to accompany them to Kabul, provided he was guaranteed *personal safety* and *money reward*; Pottinger granted this; hence—

September 20—*the prisoners were restored at Kabul* to their countrymen.

October 1842. Having *destroyed most of the fortifications of Kabul*, the *British army* proceeded unhampered through *Khyber Pass* into the *Peshawar territories*; at *Firuzpur*, the Sikh Commander-in-Chief played host to Pottinger.

Late 1842. Army under *Sir Charles Napier* advanced *against amirs of Sind* (the army was formed partly of the Kandahar regiments and partly of *fresh troops sent from Bengal and Bombay*). Depot, *Sukkur on the Indus* (in Sind).—Desperate attack by the *Baluchi cavalry* on *residence* of *Colonel, Outram political agent at Hyderabad*; Outram barely escaped to camp of *Napier*, who by then had advanced *as far as Halla.*

February 17, 1843, *battle at Miani*, near Hyderabad. Amirs with 20,000 men, Napier with about 3,000; after about three hours' *terrible fight*, Napier won, enemy fled in disorder, six amirs surrendered as prisoners, *Hyderabad at once occupied* and *plundered* (!), and the *English garrisoned the city*.

March 1843, the British garrison was reinforced with some "native" regiments from Bengal, so that Napier had about 6,000 men.

March 24, 1843. *Napier beat Sher Mohammed, Amir of Mirpur*, in action near the capital; then *city of Mirpur* seized and *sacked*! Next to be taken was *Umarkot*, a strong fort in the desert; the (Baluchi) garrison surrendered the city without drawing the sword.

June 1843, *Colonel Jacob* of the Sind Horse defeated *Sher Mohammed*, and thereby *subjugation of Sind* was *completed. Since then Sind British province, costs the Government annually more than it yields.*

Gwalior, **December 1843**. *The English troops there fighting with their ancient enemies.* This is how it came about:

1827, after advantageous treaty with Lord Hastings (1814), *Daulat Rao Sindhia died* without issue. He was *succeeded*—

1827-1843 (year of his death)—by the only heir that could be found, *Mugat Rao*, under the name of *Ali Jah Jankoji Sindhia*; left no children, only *widow 13 years old—Tara Bai*; she adopted as successor *Bhagerat Rao*, an eight-year-old child, who received the title of *Ali Jah Jyaji Sindhia*; of the two claimants to the *regency*—*Jankoji Sindhia*, called *Mama Sahib* (cf. *notes* on p. 245: *mama*=maternal uncle, *sahib*=lord), and the *steward of the household*, *Wala* (a distant relation of the deceased *Maharaja*), known as *Dada Khasji* (*dada*=a paternal grandfather, or an *elder brother—russice*[1] *дядя*[2]=uncle—and *khasji*=steward of the household), *Ellenborough* had the Resident appoint *Mama Sahib* [Regent], while *Tara Bai* was for *Dada*; hence two parties formed at court; after much confusion and some bloodshed, *Mama* was dismissed and *Dada* appointed by the *Maharani*, Tara Bai; but the *Elephant* insisted on

[1] In Russian.
[2] Written in Russian by Marx.

his *Mama*, ordered the Resident to leave Gwalior. *Dada* prepared troops to oppose the *Elephant*. Ellenborough (the Elephant) ordered *Sir Hugh Gough* to assume command of the Gwalior expedition and—

1843—to *cross the Chambal River into Sindhia territory*; the *Rani* and *Dada* thereupon offered submission, but their *army of* 60,000 *men* and *200 guns* marched out, and *drove the English beyond the Chambal* [which they had crossed].

December 29, 1843, near *Maharajpur* (in *Gwalior*), *Sir Hugh Gough* was attacked by 14,000 picked (Maratha) soldiers with numerous batteries of perfectly served artillery; Marathas fought with utmost gallantry; *the English won after heavy losses.*

December 31, 1843 The *Maharani* and *young Sindhia* came into British camp and submitted humbly; State of Gwalior was retained for *Sindhia*, the *Rani* pensioned off, the *Maratha army reduced to 6,000 men*, the *British force subsidized* [by Gwalior] *increased to 10,000 men*; Sindhia to succeed at *his majority*; meanwhile *council appointed* to manage the state affairs.

Soon after, early in 1844, the Elephant was revoked—before expiry of his term—by *Court of Directors*, because of his "*war urge*"; *Sir Henry Hardinge* was *sent* out to supersede the Elephant.

. . . .

(6) LORD HARDINGE'S ADMINISTRATION, 1844-1848

June 1844. *Hardinge arrived at Calcutta.* (He came, not as "Lord," but as *Sir Henry Hardinge*.)

1842. *Sher Singh*, one of *Ranjit Singh's* sons, *sovereign of the Punjab*; his Vizier, *Dian Singh*, induced one *Ajit Singh* to murder *Sher Singh*; but *Ajit* also murdered Sher's eldest son, *Pratap Singh*, ditto *Dian Singh himself*; the latter's brother, *Suchat*, and [son] *Hira Singh*, surrounded Lahore with troops, seized the rebels (headed by Ajit Singh), and killed them all. Thereupon *Hira Singh*, who had made himself Vizier, proclaimed [Raja] the only surviving son of Sher Singh's, viz., *Dhuleep Singh* (10 years old, gifted, the last *Maharaja* *of Lahore*). The most difficult problem for *Hira Singh* was curtailing the number or curbing the power of the *Sikh*, or *Khalsa*,[1] *army*, which indeed was the *dominant power in the state*; *Hira* fell (*done in*) as victim of a conspiracy of its officers.—A favourite of the *Rani*, the Brahmin *Lal Singh*, became Vizier; after various minor military expeditions, he found that *the only way* to pacify the Khalsa was *war against England*.

Spring 1845. The war preparations in Lahore so marked that *Sir Henry Hardinge* concentrated 50,000 men on eastern bank of Sutlej.

First Sikh War, 1845, 1846. *At end of November*, 60,000 Sikhs crossed the Sutlej and encamped on English territory near *Firuzpur*. *Governor-General Hardinge* and *Sir Hugh Gough*, his Commander-in-Chief, at once marched to oppose them. To be noted that the mishaps of the English were mostly due, besides the Sikhs' bravery, to the asinine stupidity of *Gough*, who imagined he could *do anything to the Sikhs*, in the same way as *to the easily frightened Hindus of the South, by charging them with the bayonet*.

December 18, 1845. Battle of *Mudki*, village about 20 miles from Firuzpur. *English victory* ([though] several of their "native regiments" had already given way), *Lal Singh* retired with his army during the night.

December 21, 1845. *Battle of Firuzshah*, where Sikhs had their camp. English repulsed on all sides with heavy losses.

December 22, 1845. *Resumption of battle. English won*, although with heavy losses because the *Sikhs* had not expected that after *their* "*defeat*," which to most Oriental nations means a panic and general flight, English should attack again next morning. *Sikhs retreated*, English too exhausted for pursuit. For the *attack on Lahore*, the English awaited *siege battery*, reported to be on the route *in the middle of December*; to forestall attack on the convoy by the Sikhs encamped at *Aliwal*, small village near Ludhiana—

[1] "Community," the original name of the brotherhood of Sikhs, and later the Sikh State, as well as of the soldiers' organizations, which exerted a democratic influence on the policies of the Sikh Government. Hence the Sikh feudal lords were intent on breaking the power of the Khalsa.

January 28, 1846— *battle of Aliwal*; after stubborn resistance, Sikhs driven into the river.—A few days later, the convoy arrived from Delhi in English camp.—Meanwhile the Sikhs had built very *strong fortifications*, garrisoned with nearly 40,000 men at *Sobraon*, etc., for the defence of Lahore.

February 10, 1846, *battle of Sobraon*. The Sikh army completely shattered after excellent, most courageous resistance, with *great loss on part of English*. (Much *hand-to-hand fighting*, one of the hottest actions in which the English ever engaged.) After the English had crossed the Sutlej unopposed, and occupied the strong fort of *Kasur* (not far from Lahore), *Dhuleep Singh* (the young Raja) arrived at the latter place to submit, with influential chieftains headed by *Gulab Singh* (*this fellow* was *a Rajput*, known to the English to be at heart great enemy of the Sikhs). *Treaty*, under which *country between the rivers Bias and Sutlej* to be ceded to the Company; £1,500,000 to be paid as indemnity; *Lahore* for the present to be garrisoned by the English troops.

February 20, 1846. *English army entered Lahore* in triumph. As there was no money in treasury for the payment of the £1,500,000, *Hardinge* declared *Kashmir annexed to Company*, but *Gulab Singh* offered the money, and *Kashmir* was therefore made over to him. That was how Hardinge paid his war expenses. The *troops of the Khalsa army* were paid off and disbanded; *Dhuleep Singh* was recognized as independent. *Major Henry Lawrence* left *with English garrison* at Lahore; the main army with the captured guns withdrew to Ludhiana.—*Hardinge* and *Gough* received thanks of Parliament, and were raised to peerage.—In *March 1848*, Hardinge returned to England, was succeeded as *Governor-General* by *Lord Dalhousie*.

. . . .

(7) LORD DALHOUSIE'S ADMINISTRATION, 1848-1856

April 1848. *Mulraj*, who had succeeded his father (*Sawan*) in *1844*, was deposed as *Governor of Multan* by *Dhuleep Singh*, and *Sirdar Khan*, accompanied by *Vans Agnew* (a civilian) and *Lieutenant Anderson*, was sent to take his place.

April 20, 1848. *Mulraj* handed over the keys of the city; three days after, the garrison opened the gates, Sikhs rushed in, murdered *Anderson and Vans Agnew.*—Young *Lieutenant Edwards*, stationed *near Lahore* with a *regiment of Sikhs* who began to desert, sent to *Raja of Bhawalpur* for aid, and obtained it.

May 20, 1848, he joined Colonel Courtlandt at *Dera Ghazi Khan* on the Indus; Courtlandt had 4,000 men; they were joined by *two bodies of Baluchis*, and having altogether 7,000 men, they decided to take *Multan*; after several fortunate engagements, [the English] remained before Multan till *September 1848*, when they were joined by large *English force under General Whish*; they summoned *Multan* to surrender, were refused; at the same time, *Sher Singh* (he had arrived from Lahore two months before, allegedly as ally) deserted to enemy. *Whole Punjab now in a state of revolt. Lahore Cabinet secured alliance of Dost Mohammed by promising Peshawar. Sir George Lawrence*, brother of Sir Henry, *Resident at Peshawar*; on *October 24, 1848*, Residency taken by the Sikhs, English kept close prisoners.

Second Sikh War. October 1848, Dalhousie joined the army assembled at *Firuzpur. End of October, Gough* crossed the Sutlej, joined by General Wheeler at *Jalandhar.* The Sikhs massed in the *Doab, between rivers Ravi and Chenab.*

November 22, 1848, *battle at Ramnagar.* (Sikhs under Sher Singh.) Sikhs retired beyond the *Chenab*; Gough marched north to effect a passage not in the face of the Sikh batteries.

December 2, 1848, *battle at village of Sadullapur.* (Sikhs under Sher Singh retreated towards *Jhelum* River, entrenched themselves there strongly; for six weeks, the English army inactive.

January 14,[1] 1849, *battle of Chilianwala*, village near River *Jhelum*; disastrous for English, who lost 2,300 men,

[1] January 13, according to Smith, *The Oxford History of India.*

three regiments lost their colours; they rested at Chilianwala; Sikhs retired, took up new position.

January 22, 1849, *capture of Multan by General Whish and Lieutenant Edwards* (Mulraj allowed to march out). English army marched to join *Gough*, while Lieutenant Edwards stayed at Multan with a British garrison.

January 26, 1849, *Gough's* army heard of *capture of Multan*; a few days later, *Sher Singh* offered to submit, [but English] refused.

February 12, 1849, Sher Singh made *clever flank march* in order to rush down on Lahore while whole British army in the North. *Gough* overtook him at *Gujrat*, village *near the Chenab*.

February 20, 1849, *battle of Gujrat* (British army 24,000 strong). *Comparatively bloodless victory* of the English.

March 12, 1849. *Sher Singh and his generals submitted—Dalhousie annexed Punjab* after having occupied Lahore. *Dhuleep Singh* had to place himself under British protection; Khalsa army to be disbanded; *Koh-i-noor* (diamond, cf. p. 256, n. 1) to be delivered to the fair Victoria; *the Sikh leaders' private landed possessions confiscated*; they had to regard themselves as prisoners in radius of four miles from their places of residence. *Mulraj* sentenced to life imprisonment.—*Settlement of the Punjab* left to commission headed by *Sir Henry Lawrence*, with assistance of his brother *Sir John Lawrence* (later *Governor-General*).—A *small Sikh army*, officered by English on the sepoy principle, was formed; *roads made*.

May 1849, *Gough* replaced by *Sir Charles Napier*. Quarrels between him and Dalhousie, which ended in his resignation.

1848. *Annexation of Satara*. The *Raja* from House of Shivaji, placed on throne by *Hastings* in 1818, *died*; he was childless, had on deathbed adopted a *son* and appointed him his heir. Dalhousie refused to recognize him; *annexed* [Satara].

1849-1851. Outbreaks of several hill tribes put down by *Sir Colin Campbell, Colonel Campbell, Mr. Strange*, etc. (p. 257).—A general war was declared against *dacoity, thuggee, infanticide, human sacrifices, suttee, etc.*

Second Burmese War, 1852-1853 (commenced *April 12, 1852*, ended as result of fights of *March 17 and 18, 1853*, at *Donabyu*). *Annexation of Pegu under Proclamation of December* 20, 1853.

1853. *Annexation of Berar*, where *Raja of Nagpur*, raised to throne by *Auckland* (1840), died without natural issue or adopted son.

Final Annexation of the Carnatic. In *1801*, "the Company's Nabob" had retired into private life. In *1819*, at his death, his son was put on throne, d. *1825*; his infant son then proclaimed Nabob, d. 1853,[1] and now his uncle, *Azim Jah*, claimed the title, was pensioned off, had precedence of all the other nobles in Madras, Victoria lately had given him the title of *Prince of Arcot*, fellow lives at ease in his palace at Madras.

1854.[2] *Annexation of Jhansi* (*in Bundelkhand*). The *Raja of Jhansi*, originally tributary of the Peshwa, *recognized in 1832 as independent raja, died* without natural issue, but *adopted son* living. Monsieur Dalhousie again refused to recognize him; hence rage of the dispossessed *Rani*, who later *the most prominent leader in the sepoy mutiny.*

Dandhu Panth, alias *Nana Sahib*, was the *adopted son* of the *dismissed and pensioned Peshwa Baji Rao*, who d. *1853*; Nana Sahib claimed the *annual pension of his adoptive father*—£100,000; refused. Nana submitted, later wreaked revenge on the "*English dogs.*"

1855-1856. *Outbreak of the Santals*, a half-savage tribe, in the *Rajmahal Hills* in Bengal; put down, after *seven months' guerrilla warfare*, in *February 1856.*

Early 1856, *Dalhousie declined* the "humble" request of the *deposed Raja of Mysore* to restore him in his former government.

---

[1] 1855, according to Burgess.
[2] 1853, according to Burgess.

1856. *Annexation of Oudh* because of bad government on the part of the Nabob.—*Maharaja Dhuleep Singh of the Punjab adopted Christianity. Dalhousie* withdrew, leaving a *boastful "farewell minute"*; among other things, *canals, railways, electric telegraph* built; *increase in the revenue* of *£4 million*, exclusive of annexation of Oudh; *tonnage of ships* trading to Calcutta, *nearly doubled*; in fact, *deficiency in the public accounts*, but this due to heavy expenditure for public works.—*Answer to this rodomontade*, the *Sepoy Revolution* (1857-1859).

. . . .

(8) LORD CANNING'S ADMINISTRATION, 1856-1858

February 29, 1856. *Canning assumed power.* (His *Penal Code*, alike *applicable* to *Hindus, Mohammedans, and Europeans*, not completed until *1861*.)

August 1856, *cholera*; ravaged Central India; in *Agra* alone, 15,000 deaths.

Persian War, 1856-1857. (Pam!): in *1855*, British Commissioner left *Teheran* because of "contemptuous treatment" he had met with.

1856, *Persian Government* seized *Herat* from the Afghan Isa Khan.

November 1, 1856. Canning declared war; *November* 13, several ships sailed *from Bombay* to attack *Muscat.*

Early December 1856, *Bushire* (Abu Shahr) in the Persian Gulf taken.

Meanwhile *negotiations opened* between *Sir John Lawrence* (now Chief Commissioner of Punjab in place of his brother Sir Henry) and *Dost Mohammed*, Amir of Kabul. *Early* 1857, *reconciliation, alliance, was kept.*

January 1857, *Sir James Outram* joined the *army at Bushire* as Commander-in-Chief of the expedition.

February 7, 1857, *battle of Khushab*; *about* 8,000 *Persians* completely routed by column under Outram.

February 8, 1857, *Outram* with his column returned to headquarters at Bushire.

April 1857, *capture of Mohammera.—Thereupon Treaty of Peace: Persians to withdraw for ever from Herat and Afghanistan*, to treat the British Commissioner at Teheran "with all distinction."

. . . .

1857. The Sepoy Revolt. For some years *Sepoy Army* very disorganized; *40,000 soldiers from Oudh* in it, bound together by caste and nationality; one common pulse in army, insult to a regiment on the part of its superiors felt as grievance by all the rest; officers powerless; laxity of discipline; *open acts of mutiny frequent*, suppressed with more or less difficulty; *downright refusal* of *the Bengal army to cross the sea for the attack of Rangoon*, necessitating the *substitution of Sikh regiments* (1852). (All this since *annexation of Punjab*—1849—became worse since *annexation of Oudh*—1856.) *Lord Canning* began his administration with *arbitrary act*; until then, the *sepoys of Madras and Bombay enlisted* by regulation *for service all over the world*, the *Bengalese* only for *service in India*; *Canning* made *"general service enlistment"* the *rule in Bengal*. The "fakirs" denounced this as *attempt to abolish caste*, etc.

Early 1857, (Pam's) *cartridges, lately issued, greased with the fat of pigs and cows*, expressly, said the *fakirs*, in order to *cause every sepoy to break his caste*.

Hence, *sepoy émeutes at Barrackpore* (near Calcutta) and *Raniganj* (near *Bankura*).

February 26, sepoy émeute at *Berhampore* (on *the Hooghly*, south of *Murshidabad*); in *March*, sepoy insurrection at Barrackpore; all this in *Bengal* (forcibly quelled).

March and April. *Sepoys of Ambala and Meerut set* constantly and secretly *their barracks on fire*; in *districts of Oudh and North-West*, fakirs inflamed the people against England. *Nana Sahib, Raja of Bithur* (on Ganges), plotted with *Russia, Persia, the princes of Delhi*, and the *ex-King of Oudh*, took advantage of the *sepoy disturbances* consequent upon the greased cartridges.

April 24.[1] *Rising at Lucknow* of *48th Bengalese* (Regiment), *3rd Native Cavalry, 7th Oudh Irregulars, quelled by Sir Henry Lawrence* bringing up English troops.

At Meerut (north-east of Delhi), *11th and 20th Native Infantry* attacked the English, shot their officers, fired the town, slew all English ladies and children, *went off to Delhi.*

At Delhi, in night, *some of the mutineers* galloped into Delhi, *sepoys* there rose (*54th, 74th, 38th Native Infantry*); the *English Commissioner, chaplain, officers, murdered*; nine English officers defended the magaz ne, blew it up (two[2] perished); the other *Englishmen in the city* fled to jungles, most killed by natives or severe weather; some *arrived* safely at *Meerut*, now deserted of troops. But *Delhi in insurgent hands.*

At Firuzpur, 45th and 57th Native attempted to *seize the fort*, driven off by the *61st English*; but they plundered town, set it on fire, were next day driven off by cavalry turning off the fort.

At Lahore, on news of the events at Meerut and Delhi, the *sepoys on general parade*, ordered by General *Corbett, disarmed* (surrounded *by English troops* with artillery).

May 20. *64th, 55th, 39th Native Infantry* disarmed *at Peshawar* (as at Lahore); then the *remainder of available English and faithful Sikhs* cleared the beleaguered stations of *Noushera and Mardan*, and *at end of May,* the *large station of Ambala*, garrisoned by *several European regiments* assembled from the near-by stations; collected here, *nucleus of an army under General Anson....* The *hill station of Simla*, crowded with English families resident there for the hot season, was *not attacked.*

May 25. *Anson* with his little army marched on *Delhi*; he *died* on *May 27*, replaced by *Sir Henry Barnard*; the latter on *June 7* joined by *English troops* under *General Wilson* (coming *from Meerut*; some fighting with the sepoys had taken place on the route). *Rebellion*

---

[1]May 3, according to Kaye and Malleson, *History of the Indian Mutiny*, Vol. 3, London, 1 89-1892.

[2]Five, according to Kaye and Malleson, Vol. 2.

spread throughout Hindustan; in *20 different places simultaneously, sepoy risings and murder of the English*; chief scenes: *Agra, Bareili, Moradabad. Sindhia* loyal to the "English dogs," not so his "*troopers*"; *Raja of Patiala*—for shame!—sent large body of soldiers in aid of the English! *At Mainpuri* (North-Western Provinces), a young brute of a lieutenant, one *De Kantzow,* saved treasury and fort.

At Cawnpore, June 6, 1857, Nana Sahib (had taken *command of three sepoy regiments* and *three regiments of native cavalry*, who had risen in Cawnpore, while *Sir Hugh Wheeler*, commander of Cawnpore troops, had *only one battalion of European infantry*, and had obtained a *slight reinforcement* from without; he held the *fort and the barracks*, whither all English people, women, children, had fled) *beleaguered Sir Hugh Wheeler.*

June 26, 1857. *Nana Sahib* offered safe retreat for all Europeans if *Cawnpore* delivered up; *June* 27 (Wheeler having accepted), 400 of the survivors allowed to embark in boats and proceed down the Ganges; Nana opened fire on them from both sides; one boat escaped, attacked lower down, scuttled, only four men of the whole garrison escaped. *A boat*, which had stuck fast on a sandbank, filled with *women and children*, seized, marched to Cawnpore, there shut up closely as prisoners; 14 *days later* (*in July*), more English prisoners dragged there by the insurgent sepoys from *Fatehgarh* (military station three miles from Farrukhabad).

Upon orders from Canning, troops moved from *Madras, Bombay, Ceylon*. On *May* 23, *Madras reinforcement* under *Neill* landed, and Bombay contingent up the *Indus*, proceeded to *Lahore.*

June 17, *Sir Patrick Grant* (succeeding *Anson* as *Commander-in-Chief in Bengal*) and *General Havelock*, the Adjutant General, *arrived at Calcutta*, started at once thence.

June 6, *at Allahabad, sepoys mutinied*, butchered the (English) *officers* with their wives and children, attempted to *seize the fort*, defended by *Colonel Simpson*, who on *June 11* received aid from *Colonel Neill coming up with the Madras fusiliers from Calcutta*; the latter *turned out all Sikhs, occupied the fort, garrisoned the place only with Britishers.* (On the way he had occupied *Benares* and defeated 37th Native Infantry in first stage of mutiny; *sepoys* fled); (English) *troops* flowed from all sides into Allahabad.

June 30, General *Havelock*, arriving at Allahabad, took command, marched with *some 1,000* Britishers on *Cawnpore*; *July 12*, at *Fatehpur*, repulsed the sepoys, etc., *some more actions.*

July 16, *Havelock's army on the outskirts of Cawnpore*; defeated the Indians, but was too late *to enter the citadel*; *in the night, Nana butchered all English prisoners—officers, ladies, children*; then blew up the magazine and *abandoned the town.—July 17*, English troops entered the place.—*Havelock* marched into Nana's nest, *Bithur*, took it unresisted, *destroyed the palace, blew up the fort*, then marched back to *Cawnpore*; there he left *Neill* to *garrison and hold the station*, while *Havelock* off to *relieve Lucknow*; there, despite the efforts of *Sir Henry Lawrence*, the whole city, *save the Residency*, fell into *insurgent hands.*

June 30, *whole garrison* marched out against body of rebels in vicinity; repulsed; *sheltered again in Residency*; *this place besieged.*

July 4, *Sir Henry Lawrence* died (consequent to *explosion of shell* wounding him on *July 2*); *Colonel Inglis took command*; they held out, with occasional sorties against the besiegers, *for three months.—Operations by Havelock* (p. 271). After the latter back to *Cawnpore*, *Sir James Outram* joined him with large bodies of troops, and he ditto moved up reinforcements of *many detached regiments* from various mutinous districts.

September 19, the whole force crossed the Ganges under *Havelock, Outram, and Neill*. On 23d, they stormed the *Alambagh*, the *summer palace of the Kings of Oudh*, eight miles from Lucknow.

September 25, *final rush made on Lucknow*, reached the *Residency*, where the united force had to stay, *closely blockaded, for two months more.* (*General Neill* fell during the fighting in town; *Outram* received severe wound in arm.)

September 20. *Delhi captured*, after six days of actual fighting, under *General Wilson*. (Cf. pp. 272, 273 for details.) *Hodson* at the head of his body of horse broke *into palace*, seized *old King and Queen* (*Zeenat Mahal*); they were thrown in prison, while Hodson *with his own hand killed* (by shooting) *the princes. Delhi garrisoned and quieted.* Immediately after, *Colonel Greathed* went from Delhi to *Agra*, near which he defeated a *strong body of mutineers* from Holkar's capital, *Indore*;

October 10, he took *Agra*, then proceeded to *Cawnpore*, where he arrived on *October 26*; *meanwhile* mutineers defeated at *Azamgarh*, *Chattna* (near *Hazaribagh*), *Khajwah*, and in country round Delhi, under *Captain Boileau*, *Major English*, *Peel* (the latter with *naval brigade*; also, about to enter the scene of action, *Probyn's* and *Fane's Horse*, reinforcements from home; also, *regiments of volunteers* raised), and *Showers*. *Sir Colin Campbell* in *August* took command of Calcutta, prepared to carry war on larger scale.

November 19, 1857, *Sir Colin Campbell* delivered the besieged garrison in the *Residency at Lucknow*. (*Sir Henry Havelock died on November 24*); from *Lucknow*—

November 25, 1857—*Colin Campbell* proceeded to *Cawnpore*, which town had fallen into *insurgent hands* again.

December 6, 1857. *Victorious battle by Colin Campbell at Cawnpore*; the rebels fled, leaving the town deserted, were pursued and severely cut up by *Sir Hope Grant*. In *Patiala*, *Mainpuri*, rebels defeated by *Colonel Seaton*, *Major Hodson*, respectively; and in many other places.

January 27, 1858, *King of Delhi* [brought] to court-martial under *Dawes*, etc.; sentenced to death as "felon" (representative of the Mogul dynasty, dating from 1526!) sentence commuted to *transportation for life to Rangoon*. *Conveyed* at end of the *year*.

Sir Colin Campbell's Campaign of 1858. On *January 2*, he took *Farrukhabad* and *Fatehgarh*, established himself at *Cawnpore*, whither he ordered all available troops, stores, and guns from every quarter.—*Rebels were massed about Lucknow*, where *Sir James Outram* held them at bay.—After many other incidents (cf. pp. 276, 277),

Lucknow recaptured on March 15[1] (under Colin Campbell, *Sir James Outram*, etc.); *looting* of the town, where *treasures of Oriental art stored up*; fighting over on *March 21*; last gun fired on the 23d.—*Flight of the insurgents to Bareili*, headed by *Prince Firuz*, [son of] Shah *of Delhi*, *Nana Sahib of Bithur*, the *Maulavi of Fyzabad*, and *Hazrat Mahal*, the *Begum of Oudh*.

April 25,[2] 1858. *Campbell* took *Shahjahanpur*; *Mogs* beat back attack by rebels *near Bareili*; on *May 6*, *siege guns opened on Bareili*, while *General Jones* came up by appointment after *having seized Moradabad*; *Nana* and his followers fled, *Bareili taken without resistance*. *Shahjahanpur*, meanwhile closely invested by the rebels, relieved by *General Jones*; *Lugard's division*, marching from Lucknow, attacked, suffered severely at the hands of mutineers under *Kunar Singh*; the *Maulavi of Fyzabad* killed soon afterwards, after Sir *Hope Grant* defeated the *Begum*, who fled to the *Gogra River* to rally new forces.

By mid-June 1858, mutineers defeated on all points; incapable of joint action; broken up into *bands of marauders* pressing hard the divided forces of the English. *Centres of action*: *the standards of the Begum*, the Prince of Delhi, and Nana Sahib.

Finishing stroke dealt to insurrection by Sir Hugh Rose's two months' (*May and June*) *campaign in Central India*.

January 1858, Rose took *Rathgarh*, in *February*, *Sangur and Garrakota*, marched on *Jhansi*, where the Rani had taken her stand.

April 1, 1858, severe action against *Tantia Topi*, cousin of *Nana Sahib*, who advanced from *Kalpi* to protect *Jhansi*; Tantia defeated.

April 4,[3] *Jhansi taken*; the Rani and Tantia Topi escaped, awaited the English at *Kalpi*; while *marching thither*—

---

[1] March 14, according to Kaye and Malleson, Vol. 4.
[2] April 30, according to Kaye and Malleson, Vol. 4.
[3] April 5, according to Kaye and Malleson, Vol. 4.

May 7, 1858—*Rose* attacked by strong body of the enemy at the *town of Kanya*; he signally defeated them.

May 16, 1858, *Rose within a few miles of Kalpi*, closely invested the mutineers.

May 22, 1858, desperate *sortie* by the mutineers from Kalpi; they were worsted, fled;

May 23, 1858, *Rose occupied Kalpi*. Remained there few days for rest of his soldiers, who worn out [by campaign] and hot summer.

June 2, *young Sindhia* (English dog-man) driven out of *Gwalior* by his troops after hard fighting, fled for his life to Agra. Rose marched on *Gwalior*; the *Rani of Jhansi*[1] and *Tantia Topi* at head of the rebels gave him—

June 19—*battle at the Loshkar Hill* (*before Gwalior*); *Rani* killed, her army dispersed after much slaughter. *Gwalior in English hands.*

During July, August, and September, 1858, *Sir Colin Campbell, Sir Hope Grant, and General Walpole* engaged to hunt down the more prominent rebels and take *all forts* whose possession disputed; *the Begum made some final stands*, then fled *with Nana Sahib across the Rapti River* to the territories of the English dog-man, *Jang Bahadur of Nepal*; he allowed the English to pursue the rebels into his country, thus the "last bands of desperadoes dispersed"; *Nana* and the *Begum fled into the hills*, while their followers laid down their arms.

Early 1859, *Tantia Topi's* hiding-place detected, he tried and executed.—*Nana Sahib* is "supposed" to have died in Nepal. *Khan of Bareili* was seized and shot; *Mammu Khan* of *Lucknow* sentenced to life imprisonment; others transported or imprisoned for various terms; *bulk of the rebels*—their regiments disbanded—laid down the sword, *became ryots. The Begum of Oudh* lived at Khatmandu in *Nepal.*

Confiscation of the soil of Oudh, which Canning declared to be the property of the Anglo-Indian Government! Sir Robert Montgomery made *Chief Commissioner of Oudh* in place of Sir James Outram.

---

[1] Her name was Lakshmi Bai.

Abolition of the East India Company. It was broken even before the war [was] at an end.

December 1857. *Palmerston's India Bill*; *first reading passed* despite solemn protest by *the Board of Directors in February* 1858, but Liberal Ministry replaced by Tory.

February 19, 1858, *Disraeli's India Bill* (cf. p. 281) fell through.

August 2, 1858, *Lord Stanley's India Bill passed*, and thereby *finis of the East India Co*. India a *province of the empire of the "great" Victoria*!

INDEX[1]

[1] Geographical names are italicized—*Ed.*

C

D